The Definitive Authority
on **Solution Selling**

THE KEEPING FUNNEL FULL

Don Thomson

Edited by Pam Withers
Design by Artemis PR & Design

Printed in Canada by Friesen Printers, Altona, Manitoba

First Printing: October 2004
Second Printing: June 2005

Library and Archives of Canada Cataloguing in Publication

Thomson, Don, 1936-

    Keeping the Funnel Full: The Definitive Authority on Solution Selling / Don Thomson.

Includes index.

ISBN 0-9735790-0-5

1. Industrial marketing. 2. Selling. I. Title.

HF5438.25.T46 2004   658.8'04   C2004-903341-7

Mardon Publishing Inc.
French Creek, British Columbia

ORDERING THE BOOK

If you would like to order additional copies of KEEPING THE FUNNEL FULL, visit www.keepingthefunnelfull.com.

CONTENTS

List of Figures

DEDICATION

A special acknowledgement to my wife, Mary, who read through the drafts of each section as they were written and helped make the messages clearer to the reader. Mary's contribution was highlighted by my editor's comment, made after reading ten pages of the manuscript: "I see this as a pretty healthy patient needing only light substantive editing."

ACKNOWLEDGEMENTS

I owe a great deal to the old Neely Sales Region of Hewlett Packard (HP) for setting me straight on how to hire, train, and coach outstanding sales professionals. Many people have referred to the Neely Sales Organization as one of the best sales rep organizations in America. Former President Bill Hewlett clearly thought so: he bought it in the 1960s to serve as Hewlett Packard's western sales region. Mike Leavell, my regional sales manager in the Neely Sales Region, played hardball, but was always fair and supportive. I would also like to acknowledge my Neely district sales manager, John Kemper, who gave me a career in sales management.

Fran Moynihan, my regional sales manger at Pyramid Technology, coached me in many sales strategies, not just because he wanted to help, but because he loved strategizing. His coaching style for brainstorming sales strategies was uncanny. To my mind, he was the best sales manager a sales professional could ever want.

My sincere thanks to Suzanne Bowen, Ken Merkley, Marilynne Miles Gray, Bruce McGibbon, Ian Ferguson, Darren Stanger, Garry Sedun, Tom Zaban, David McMillan, Michelle van den Broek, Lyndon Olson, Dave Slater, and Colin Lennox for making numerous suggestions as it developed. The idea for writing this book came from the late Colin Lennox of the Vancouver Island Advanced Technology Centre. Every two or three months during the writing, Colin would call to see how the book was progressing. His inspiration during this period was invaluable. Ian Ferguson of the WCG International Consultants Ltd. was a huge supporter and a motivating force. Bill Jackson was invaluable in making the book an easier patient for the designer.

Particular thanks go to Christina Harris of Artemis PR & Design Inc., who designed the covers and the book layout. I am delighted that Pam Withers became my official editor. She is an accomplished author in her own right, having written half a dozen books, including some best sellers, in addition to editing nonfiction books.

Most important of all, thousands of people and hundreds of prospects and customers provided the material and all the stories presented in KEEPING THE FUNNEL FULL. For that, I thank you.

Don Thomson
September 30, 2004

FOREWORD

Selling has been my profession for 35 years and I've had the opportunity to work with many highly skilled and successful sales professionals during that time.

Don Thomson is unique among that group!

KEEPING THE FUNNEL FULL details a wide range of time-tested processes, tactics, and strategies that will enable any sales representative to obtain more meetings and close more business. Using real life experiences from his career, Thomson bridges the gap between the clinical "how to" and the "overly simplistic" approaches to this topic. The Charlotte story is an example of a major victory thanks to some common sense and flexible action while being level locked throughout the campaign.

The author brings more to the topic than a formula – he brings a lifelong passion for selling, a true respect for the customer, and a dedication to being prepared for any surprise in a campaign. It is no accident that Don has exceeded his sales quota every year of his career.

The concept of empowering the screening source is vintage Thomson at his best – a chapter worth the price of the book, and a process that Don developed uniquely and still practices to this day.

Read the book, absorb the content, implement the concepts, make more sales, enhance your career, and watch your FUNNEL grow!

Fran Moynihan
Vice President, Sales
FUJITSU TRANSACTION SOLUTIONS INC.

AUTHOR'S PREFACE

KEEPING THE FUNNEL FULL is based entirely on my thirty-year selling career of exceeding quota and belonging to that prestigious 20% club each and every year. I believe the ideas presented in this book will go a long way towards helping sales professionals enjoy membership in that club.

Selling to corporations is difficult, because every prospect requires a different approach. No two sales are the same. To compound the problem, for every rule, there are exceptions. Why does 20% of the sales force often account for 80% of the revenue? You'll find the answers in KEEPING THE FUNNEL FULL.

Not all the topics presented are for everyone, but there is something of value for every sales professional, be they new to selling or a seasoned veteran. The Prospecting Process (Part 2) and the Selling Process (Part 3) are for everyone, because they contain the essence of solution selling. You may even want to start reading the book from Part 2. If your company is already using an effective sales force automation system, I do not advocate replacing it. However, if you wish to develop your own system, you might consider adopting some of the concepts presented in the FUNNEL Design Workshop (Part 4).

Compare the information in this book to spring training for baseball players. Every year, players attend training camps to hone their professional skills. Many salespeople start out doing the same, but lose the habit over time. Once they've read KEEPING THE FUNNEL FULL, I believe they'll feel inspired to resurrect those sales activities that worked successfully for them in the past.

The Author's First Sale

"Are outstanding sales professionals born or created?" Many people will do well selling to corporations, providing they have the right attitude and are willing to work hard to understand the profession. But only a few have an innate ability to sell from a very early age.

This story has been told so many times by my mother that it has become a family legend, but all I remember is the man and his Shetland pony. Just before my third birthday, I was playing on the sidewalk with several other young boys when a man came along, leading this small pony and carrying chaps and a big white ten-gallon hat. He urged the children to persuade their parents to pay $5.00 for a large photo of their child sitting on this pony, wearing the chaps and hat. When I asked my mother, she told me that we couldn't afford it. I went back to the man with the pony and asked him to put the hat and chaps on me and place me in the saddle. I then had him walk the horse up the ten steps to our front veranda and ring the doorbell. When my mother opened the door, he asked her if she would like to have a photo of her Donald on the pony. How could she refuse? And this is how I closed my first sale.

BOOK OUTLINE

Who Should Read This Book?

KEEPING THE FUNNEL FULL is written for sales professionals who sell to small, medium or large corporations. There is something in this book for every sales professional, whether they work for a very small company or a multinational organization.

Part 1: FUNNEL Introduction

A short explanation of how the FUNNEL system works.

Part 2: The Prospecting Process

A six-step proven prospecting process on converting leads into prospects, including a surefire method to obtain appointments with Senior Executives.

Part 3: The Selling Process

Focuses on converting prospects into customers, paying particular attention to how to close a prospect stuck near the middle of the FUNNEL.

Part 4: FUNNEL Design Workshop

A train-the-trainer approach to help sales management lead a FUNNEL Design Workshop. It features two templates very useful to sales organizations.

PART 1:
FUNNEL INTRODUCTION

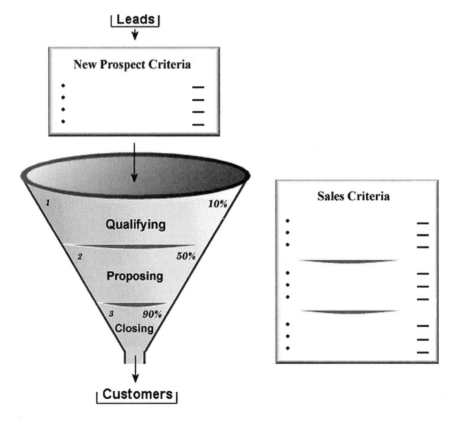

1. The Greatest Sales Tool

What makes the FUNNEL concept so profound is that it permits sales professionals to assess their entire sales program in one or two minutes. A picture is worth a thousand words. To implement the FUNNEL system successfully, it must be easy to use and on-line. This book will show you how to achieve both. Companies utilizing the FUNNEL typically have two to seven Phases. In Part 1, a three-Phase FUNNEL introduces the FUNNEL concept. In Part 4, the FUNNEL Design Workshop utilizes a four-Phase FUNNEL because it is the most common size for small to medium-sized companies.

> The FUNNEL system permits rapid review of your entire sales program

Envision the following:

- an inexhaustible supply of leads existing "above" the FUNNEL

- a number of qualified leads that have become prospects residing in the "top," "middle," or "bottom" of the FUNNEL

- a smaller number of prospects exiting the "bottom" of the FUNNEL to become customers "below" the FUNNEL (Figure 1).

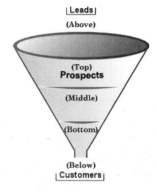

Figure 1
FUNNEL Description

> The prospecting process converts leads into prospects

2. Why a FUNNEL?

Companies often use the term pipeline to describe the flow of prospects. The problem with this is that most people regard a pipeline as having a constant diameter – in other words, all prospects entering the pipeline emerge at the other end. Experienced sales professionals who have deliberately abandoned prospects early in the sales cycle, or who have lost orders, know this is not realistic. When a prospect is abandoned for any reason during the selling process, they basically leave the so-called pipeline sideways. If, then, some prospects at the pipeline's entry point never come out its other end, the pipeline fails as a successful

Figure 2
Ideal FUNNEL Model

If you are going to lose, lose early

analogy. Far more logical is to envision a FUNNEL with horizontal pipes, to represent the flow of prospects during the selling process.

The pipes, of course, represent the abandoned prospects and lost orders flowing sideways out of the FUNNEL (Figure 2). What is one of the most painful experiences for a sales professional? Losing an order when the prospect is near the bottom of the FUNNEL. This is why it is so important to ruthlessly qualify prospects when they are near the top of the FUNNEL. If you are going to lose, lose early.

3. Benefits of the FUNNEL

- Graphically represents the current state of the sales professionals sales program including where each prospect is in the sales cycle.

- Reflects your customers' needs and your ideal selling process.

- Defines the criteria to convert leads into prospects (new prospect criteria).

- Defines the criteria to convert prospects into customers (sales criteria).

- Shows how many prospects are needed in each Phase to achieve quota, i.e. balanced FUNNEL.

- Allows comparison of your current FUNNEL with the balanced FUNNEL so it becomes evident which sales criteria need to be satisfied.

- Assists in determining the next steps to be taken in the sales process.

- Highlights what prospects should be abandoned.

- Hastens the productivity of newly hired sales professionals.

- Shows how your territory and prospects are developing through monthly copies of your FUNNEL.

- Generates an accurate sales forecast because each Phase is weighted.

- Becomes the core component of the FUNNEL template.

4. FUNNEL Concept

The FUNNEL approach is powerful because it shows at a glance the status of all your prospects and where they are in the sales cycle. The size and shape of the FUNNEL reflects the complexity of the selling process used to sell your company's products.

#	Phase	Sales Criteria	Completed
1	Qualifying	Needs assessment done	x
		Approver identified	x
		Coach candidate identified	x
		Funding budgeted	x
2	Proposing	Demo given	x
		Coach developed	x
		Competition identified	x
		Proposal submitted	
3	Closing	Approver on-side	x
		All issues satisfied	x
		Order received	

Figure 3 Three-Phase FUNNEL – Sales Criteria

The FUNNEL is segmented into a number of logically linked Phases. A specific set of sales criteria, unique for each company, is associated and aligned with each Phase. The overall summary of sales criteria for all Phases serves as a close approximation of your company's ideal sales process. Both the Phases and the sales criteria within each Phase follow a chronological order. When sales criteria for a given Phase have been completed or satisfied, you have earned the right

When all sales criteria are satisfied in previous and current Phases, the prospect moves to the next Phase

> **A prospect becomes a customer when it exits the bottom of the FUNNEL**

> **The percentage probability of closing increases as the prospect moves down the FUNNEL**

to move that prospect down into the next Phase. The same rule applies as the prospect moves downward to each subsequent Phase. The prospect continues flowing downward in this fashion until it either exits out the bottom as a customer or moves sideways as a lost or abandoned order. If even one sales criterion in Phase 1 is not satisfied, the prospect cannot be moved to Phase 2 – important in that this omission often identifies the major reason why a prospect is stuck in the FUNNEL. Why might you abandon a prospect? When a Senior Executive confirms he or she has no budget for the project. The status of the sales criteria in all the Phases reflects where each prospect is in the sales cycle. Prospects become customers when they exit the bottom of the FUNNEL.

Percentage Probability and Sale Forecast

The percentage probability improves the accuracy of the sales forecast by weighting each Phase with a percentage. The percentage probability assigned to each subsequent Phase should increase because as the prospect moves downward to the next Phase it means more sales criteria have been satisfied. These percentages are not based on any mathematical model. Phase 1 may be assigned a probability of 10% while the last Phase may be given a probability of 90%. Because a new prospect entering Phase 1 is required only to pass the new prospect criteria, it may not have satisfied any of the sales criteria associated with Phase 1. That's why many companies believe that the percentage probability of Phase 1 should be low. The best strategy, of course, is to have your design team determine what percentage probability is realistic for selling your company's products.

To achieve a more accurate sales forecast, use percentage probabilities instead of giving the same weight to each prospect in the FUNNEL. And definitely avoid the dangerous practice of assigning percentages not based on a specific set of sales criteria. A typical example is the sales person who, based only on intuition, tells his manager that the deal is 80% done. Sales forecasts based on well thought-out sales criteria always produce greater accuracy. Every sales professional in your company should be using the same percentage probabilities to denote the completion of specific criteria otherwise these percentages are meaningless.

New Prospect Criteria	Status
Researched company	x
Sense of urgency	
Verifies a possible fit	
Face-to-face meeting	

Figure 4 New Prospect Criteria

New Prospect Criteria

The purpose of the new prospect criteria is to establish a corporate standard for leads entering the top of the FUNNEL (Figure 4). No prospect should appear in the FUNNEL until it has passed the new prospect criteria. This prevents companies from committing valuable resources prematurely. The key is to complete the number of prospecting calls, phone calls, and research needed until the new prospect criteria have been satisfied. Each company should customize its own new prospect criteria.

5. The Balanced FUNNEL

Sales professionals want to know how many prospects and how much revenue is needed in each Phase to obtain or exceed quota. This status is referred to as a Balanced FUNNEL. Figure 5 represents a three-Phase Balanced FUNNEL populated with sufficient prospects to ensure consistent sales quota performance. Each dot represents a prospect.

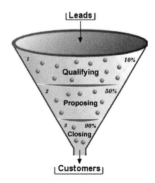

Figure 5
Balanced Three-Phase FUNNEL

A Balanced FUNNEL
is populated with
sufficient prospects to
achieve quota

Because your goal is to lose early if you must lose, you clearly need more prospects in Phase 1 than in Phase 2. Usually the FUNNEL lacks space to represent all your prospects by full company name, so consider representing them with an alphanumeric code that suggests their identity. For example, list ABC Company as ABC. Use a spreadsheet if you have too many prospects to fit into a FUNNEL diagram. (A dilemma we'd all like to have more often!)

6. The Accurate Sales Forecast

A percentage probability
always results in more
accurate sales forecasts

Once you have loaded your FUNNEL, you'll know where each prospect is in its sales cycle. Now, using percentage probabilities, compute how many prospects are needed in each Phase to achieve quota. That's easy! And remember, sales forecasts based on percentage probability (as opposed to those that give the same weight to every prospect) result in more accurate sales forecasts.

7. Managing Your Sales Program

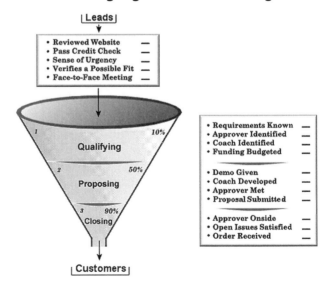

Figure 6 Three-Phase FUNNEL template

By updating and reviewing your FUNNEL on a regular basis, you will become fully knowledgeable about the status of your sales program. Why not have the most recent copy of your FUNNEL close at hand? It doesn't matter whether it is on the inside front cover of your hard-copy notebook, or in your computer, laptop, or personal digital assistant (PDA), as long as it is readily available.

Review your FUNNEL templates while waiting for planes or between sales calls. The more frequently you review the FUNNEL template, the more ideas you will generate for updating your strategies to close new sales.

8. Key Points

- The FUNNEL is the best shape for representing the flow of prospects during the sales cycle.

- When you are implementing a new FUNNEL system, pass all your perceived prospects through the new prospect criteria to verify that they are still prospects.

- The number of Phases and the sets of sales criteria in your FUNNEL are a direct measure of the complexity of your selling process.

- When all sales criteria have been satisfied in the previous and current Phases, move the prospect down to the next Phase.

- Strive continually to grow your FUNNEL into a Balanced FUNNEL that allows you to achieve your sales quota.

- Be ruthless in evaluating leads with the new prospect criteria.

- After one or two prospecting calls, abandon leads that don't satisfy the new prospect criteria.

- Use percentage probabilities for a more accurate sales forecast.

- Review your prospecting program frequently by keeping your accurate sales forecast template and the FUNNEL template of each lead and prospect in your hard-copy notebook and computer.

- Use the FUNNEL system as your planning tool to join the top 20% club.

- For in-depth information, check out the FUNNEL Design Workshop in Part 4.

Notes

Notes

PART 2:
THE PROSPECTING PROCESS

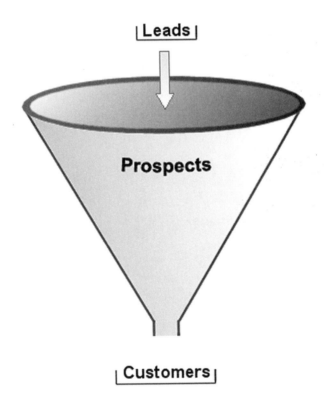

9. Introduction

Part 2 makes prospecting easier. What is the prospecting process? It's the steps needed to convert leads located above the FUNNEL into prospects located in the FUNNEL – something that occurs when the new prospect criteria have been satisfied. Prospecting calls include all face-to-face calls that determine whether a lead can be converted into a prospect. This is a fact-finding mission and not an opportunity to sell your products.

Be prepared to give a short overview about your company on this prospecting call, but leave that as your last agenda item unless you are asked for it. First calls are all about learning the needs of the prospect. Sometimes where the issues are complex, it may be necessary to make more than one call, or to call on others in the company to fully understand the needs. Once prospects know you understand their needs, you've earned the right to request a presentation.

> **Once prospects know you understand their needs, you've earned the right to request a product presentation**

In order to keep the top of your FUNNEL full, make a point of finding three new prospects in the days immediately following a sale, above and beyond normal prospecting.

> **Make a point of finding three new prospects in the days following a sale**

While first prospecting calls can't always be on a Senior Executive, that is the best place to start. If circumstances require you to call on a lower-level manager, endeavor to meet the appropriate Senior Executive as early as possible; otherwise you may find yourself level locked. Consider whether it's appropriate to ask about being introduced to a Senior Executive, because if you get a negative answer from this lower-level manager and still go upstairs, you lower your chances of winning business from this firm.

> **Constantly look for opportunities to be introduced to Senior Executives**

Looking for an effective introduction to a Senior Executive? Have a Senior Executive of an existing customer do the honors. This is an excellent way to open doors.

While the prospecting process is one of the most difficult aspects of selling, seasoned sales professionals learn to excel at it because they recognize it is key to keeping their FUNNELS full. By prospecting continuously, you keep the top of the FUNNEL full so that you can close orders continuously in the months ahead. Prospecting is hard work but the payoff is enormous.

Earning the Right

During prospecting and selling, you'll ask many questions and request many actions of the people you are meeting. If you ask or request these prematurely, you may be viewed as an overly aggressive sales person. Timing is everything. For every question you ask and action you request, you must first ask yourself:

Earn the right to make a request or take an action

> "Have I earned the right to ask this question or request that action?"

10. Creating a Low-Risk Image

Prospective customers who regard you as an unknown company, product, or salesperson may feel it is too risky to get involved. Combat that by developing a low-risk image – namely, take the time to court them.

Frequent Contact

You don't need to call on your new prospective customers daily or even weekly, but do determine the magic number of calls per week or month that will put them at ease. Once your prospective customer views your company as a viable alternative, ask how frequently they would like to meet with you. If they suggest once every two weeks, do so even if it means flying a couple of hundred miles. (Regional jets make that easy.) This strategy is effective particularly when selling in a remote location where the current vendor has local sales presence and regular meetings with customers.

Here's a sample first meeting.

"Ms. Green, I feel these meetings have been productive for both of us. Don't you agree?"

"Yes I do, Tony. I'm currently meeting with our vendor's sales rep every two weeks."

"Ms. Green, would you like to meet every two weeks?"

"Let's do it."

"What day of the week works best for you? I'd like to fly down in the morning."

"Let's do it Wednesdays at 10:30 in the morning starting in two weeks."

By meeting you every two weeks, Ms. Green will begin to feel more comfortable doing business with you. As you lower her sense of risk, you can begin to meet less often, perhaps monthly and then quarterly. But by all means continue meeting your prospect even after they become a customer, and beware letting the frequency drop too far. Annual get-togethers may make you vulnerable to losing Ms. Green to a competitor.

Timely Response

Phone a prospective customer, and you may not get a response for weeks. But when they call you, they expect their calls to be returned within a day or two. Leave it for a week, and they'll likely opt for your competitors.

Appearance and Behavior

Dress for the occasion and the persons you are meeting. Professors, for instance, do not appreciate salespeople calling on them wearing $1,000 suits. They feel more comfortable when the sales person is dressed more in keeping with university attire. Dress for your audience.

Know Your Products

Never make calls on prospective customers without a sound knowledge of your own company's products and policies. It is expensive to bring a technical person on prospecting calls to cover for your lack of product knowledge. There is more to being a competent sales professional than sound product knowledge, but even the most talented rep will get nowhere without it.

Know Your Client's Organization

It is critical that you know your client's organization both from the viewpoints of the reporting structure and the influence structure. That means checking a client's website for the names of key executives, their titles and responsibilities, and/or visiting your city's central library for business directories, which typically include the names and titles of key executives, mailing and e-mail addresses, and phone numbers. The most effective way to obtain the organization chart is to ask for it from your prospective prospect once you feel you have earned the right to ask this question.

Use Your Resources Appropriately

Generally speaking, a sales professional should never take a technical support person on prospecting calls. The last thing a small company with only one or two technical people wants is its products delayed because designers are tied up on too many joint prospecting calls. Make an exception, however, when the prospective customer indicates that they will have a technical person, such as the Chief Technology Officer, attend the meeting.

Understand Your Prospect's Issues

Here's a good starting point: Carefully formulate an agenda and a list of questions that will elicit the prospect's issues and concerns, its corporate pain, and the names of others you should meet. By presenting an agenda, you show that you are organized and you enable the prospective customer to clearly understand the objectives of the meeting. And there's little or no need to modify the agenda for it to serve all your first prospecting calls. Every company with an outside sales force should spend a one- or two-hour workshop developing the agenda and list of questions for the prospecting calls; it will benefit the entire sales force.

11. Sources of Prospects

There are many sources of prospects, but the most productive are often well-planned seminars. Others include:

Seminars are often the best source of new prospects

- existing customers (ask them)

- leads and prospects (ask them)

- direct mailers

- referrals

- consulting companies

- service and support people assigned to the account

- non-competing sales professionals

- professional or targeted industry organizations

- websites (yours and others)

- trade shows

- networking events

- newspapers and trade magazine articles

- surveys

A small geographical information systems (GIS) company with revenues of $100K per month was struggling with fifty employees and seven salespeople. In the past, the firm had spent its budget of $75K exclusively on space advertising in targeted trade magazines. When the advertising and sales promotion manager was asked how much business could be attributed to this investment, he didn't have a clue. When the new sales and marketing vice president got wind of this, he lost no time convincing the CEO that the $75K should be invested in a prospect seminar program designed for 200 potential customers in three key cities. After three months of planning, the company delivered three seminars to more than 700 attendees – pre-empting the need for any further prospecting for six months, and allowing the sales force to focus entirely on closing new business. The monthly revenue stream soon increased to $400K, transposing a struggling company to a highly profitable one, even after the firm reduced its sales force from seven to four sales professionals. What a difference a viable seminar program can make!

12. Prospecting Seminars

Because savvy sales professionals recognize prospecting seminars as their most important source of prospects, we'll cover this topic in true depth.

Audience

Avoid mixing Senior Executives with lower-level management

If you don't want to court disaster, do not mix Senior Executives with low- to middle-level management at the same seminar. Otherwise, you satisfy neither. Senior Executives focus on high-level financial and strategic issues, while low- to middle-management are more interested in the applications and benefits of products. So consider holding two seminars, one for each audience, preferably serving Senior Executives first, as they are a valuable source of suggestions for who should be invited to the more detailed product seminar.

Selecting Dates

Schedule seminars on Tuesdays or Thursdays

Beyond the availability of the venue and guest speaker, there are several considerations to take into account when selecting dates for your seminars.

- Avoid Mondays and Fridays, since employees frequently tap them as days off for three day week-ends.

- Avoid Wednesdays to accommodate executives on business trips, which are typically Monday to Wednesday or Wednesday to Friday. So, schedule your seminars on Tuesdays or Thursdays!

- Select a date that avoids major city events that may divert potential attendees.

- Avoid the weeks either side of statutory holidays such as Easter, Thanksgiving, or Christmas. Especially at Thanksgiving, you'll be lucky to fill any room.

Mailing Lists and Telesales

Tap mailing lists to specific industries or markets for your products. Although a telesales campaign based on mailing lists is expensive, it's effective for attracting large audiences. Normally you are authorized to use purchased mailing lists only once. If you lack the staff to do telesales yourself, contract the job to automated telesales companies with a strong track record, but don't forget to ensure an adequate sales force is in place to follow-up on all the leads generated in a timely manner, or you may as well have no prospects at all.

Handouts

Registrants appreciate a handout package as they sign in. Copies of presentation slides should be bound in a workbook, the lower half of each page left available for note taking. The speakers' biographies should be bound into the workbook immediately after the title page, as attendees like to read this information while waiting for the seminar to start. Foolishly place this information at the back of the binder for modesty's sake and guess what? Many of the attendees will never see it. As for the agenda and blank seminar evaluation forms, insert them loosely just inside the front cover of the workbook.

> **Leave the lower half of handout pages for note taking**

Handout packages can include corporate and product brochures, customer profiles, news releases, newspaper articles, and presentation material. But one caution: Most corporate and product brochures are too expensive to distribute to attendees. They'll just get trashed. So consider scaling back on brochures, saving them for sales calls after the attendees become prospects.

Format for Senior Executives

Seminars are a great way of targeting Senior Executives, especially when held in an upscale venue. No need to charge an admission fee. Just limit the event to two and a half to three hours, with a coffee break, as Senior Executives can't afford the luxury of being away from their offices longer. If you must schedule a full-day seminar, expect a sharp decline in the number of registrants.

Here's a recommended format:

- Company introduction by your Senior Executives (15 minutes)

- Presentation on product benefits (30 minutes)

- Short testimonial from a customer (5 minutes)

- Coffee break (15 minutes)

- Guest speaker's presentation (45 to 60 minutes)

- The guest speaker should be an added value, a drawing card, even if this proves expensive to your firm. Schedule the guest speaker towards the end of the agenda; otherwise, you will lose attendees after the coffee break.

- Wrap-up and questions (5-15 minutes)

Format for Technical Management

Below is a suggested format for a half-day seminar aimed at a technical audience, although, depending on the content, a full-day format can also work. If possible, deliver within weeks of the Senior Executive's seminar. Again, keep it admission-free and schedule keynote speakers after the last coffee break.

Senior Executives can't afford to be away from their offices all day

- Company introduction – sales professional or sales manager (5-10 minutes)
- Technical product presentation (60 minutes)
- Customer reference presentation (20 minutes)
- Coffee break (15 minutes)
- Product demonstration (45 minutes)
- Wrap-up and questions (20 minutes)

Here's an example of a live demonstration that took some practicing and coordination, but proved very effective. It involved a GIS product with the significant benefit of being able to develop an application quickly. As the product manager was developing the application in real time, a colleague projected the Windows application onto a large screen, while the VP Engineering narrated its development according to a predetermined script.

Seminar Implementation Plans

The best way to manage all the details associated with running a successful seminar is to document them beforehand. The following seminar implementation plan accomplishes this nicely (Figure 7).

Provided they gain useful knowledge during the seminar, attendees will be interested in meeting with you in the weeks following the seminar for that important first prospecting call.

Setting and achieving interim registration quotas is motivational and rewarding. For a target of 200 attendees, consider interim registration goals. It is much easier to achieve a target of 200 attendees with these milestones. Registering people is where persistence comes into play. Leave messages only on the first phone call; otherwise you'll be labeled a pest.

Two to five percent of registrants will always cancel the week before the seminar. Consider placing people on a wait list, and confirming their seat as cancellations occur.

#	Activity	Completion Date	Done
1	Strike a planning committee	May 25	
2	Set goal of 200+ attendees	May 25	
3	Arrange for two customers to give testimonials	May 31	
4	Book seminar room	May 31	
5	Develop agenda	June 5	
6	Design electronic brochure and post to website	June 15	
7	Contract with a telesales company	June 25	
8	Purchase appropriate industry mailing lists	June 27	
9	Update your prospect database	June 30	
10	Develop an on-line seminar registration system	July 7	
11	Commence contractor's telesales campaign	July 15	
12	Design newspaper advertisement	July 31	
13	Obtain first milestone of 50 registrants	July 31	
14	Obtain second milestone of 50 additional registrants	August 21	
15	Run newspaper advertisements	August 21	
16	Commence your own company's telesales campaign	August 24	
17	Develop live demo	September 15	
18	Obtain third milestone of 50 additional registrants	September 15	
19	Prepare seminar evaluations	September 20	
20	Dry-run demo to marketing and sales force	September 27	
21	Obtain fourth milestone of 50 additional registrants	October 1	
22	E-mail reminder notice and include agenda	October 1	
23	Prepare handout packages	October 3	
24	Prepare computerized name badges	October 3	
25	Inspect venue facilities	October 6	
26	Execute seminar	October 7	
27	Evaluate seminar evaluations	October 8	
28	Create a follow-up schedule	October 8	
29	All leads to be visited within 30 days of the seminar	November 7	
30	Achieve goal of qualifying 20 new prospects (10%)	November 30	

Figure 7 Prospect Seminar Implementation Plan

Try to leverage other sales or marketing activities around your seminar, perhaps arranging meetings or a golf game the following day for certain prospects or customers (repeat business) attending from out of town.

You are well on your way to having a successful seminar once you have reserved the seminar room, booked the guest speaker, and developed the implementation plan.

Seminar Evaluation

The seminar evaluation form should tell you what worked and what didn't (Figure 8). Design questions to elicit yes or no answers by allowing the attendees to insert a checkmark. (They are reluctant to write long answers).

The Selling Process
October 7, 200X

Did you benefit from the seminar? Yes__ No__

What was the most useful tip you learned from the seminar?

_____

_____

What was the least useful tip you learned from the seminar?

_____

_____

How could the seminar be improved?

_____

_____

Did the presenters allow adequate time for discussion? Yes__ No__

Did you benefit from the customer relationship management presentation?
Yes__ No__

Would you like to receive a copy of the CRM white paper? Yes__ No__

On a scale of 1-10, with 10 being outstanding, what number would you use to rank the usefulness of this seminar? __

Would you like to be invited to our next seminar? Yes__ No__

Figure 8 Seminar Evaluation Form
Continued on next page

Would you like to be contacted by one of our sales professionals? Yes__ No__
Other comments?

_____

_____

Name: _____ (Please Print)
Thank you for completing this evaluation.

For prospect seminars, design the questions to discover what the attendees liked and didn't like. Include a few questions that give you an opportunity to make contact with them. Completed evaluations reveal both important information about potential prospects, and insights into how to improve your seminars.

Seminar Results

As we've said, prospect seminars have proven to be one of the most effective sources for finding new prospects. Many a company has gleaned most of its prospects from seminars. So if you want to fill the top of your FUNNEL, give serious consideration to launching a seminar program.

Successful execution requires lots of work and a well thought-out implementation plan. Many companies opt for holding seminars on a quarterly basis, as a principal method of sourcing new prospects. One district sales manager I know, assigns a sales professional to organize a seminar each quarter, targeted to Senior Executives in financial institutions. These typically draw 100 to 200 registrants, thanks largely to their efforts to book a keynote speaker well known in the industry. The sales professionals in that firm are never short of new prospects.

A computer company in business for less than a year touted an extremely fast parallel processor computer system with an average selling price of $250,000. The firm's president, who was the sole person responsible for sales, sold ten systems to eight companies during the first year. After two of these companies became outstanding references, he hired three sales professionals in the second year, but they experienced difficulty finding new prospects. So, the president decided to stage a half-day prospecting seminar, hoping to fill an upscale venue with 400+ attendees. With no local marketing staff, the president and his sales force worked many evenings to execute the implementation plan. Their drawing card was the guest speaker, a well-known executive from a major database company. They also arranged for one of the company's customers to address the audience on how its parallel processor computer system, coupled with this database, outperformed the competition by a factor of two during benchmark evaluations. The results of this seminar were staggering. The fledgling firm fielded an order for a $300,000 system within six weeks of the seminar. More significantly, each sales professional had so many qualified leads that the company's sales tripled during the next twelve months. The president couldn't imagine any other way that he could have achieved such results.

13. New Prospect Criteria

Every company's sales force should use a corporate standard to convert leads into prospects – new prospect criteria is unique to each sales force (Figure 9). We've defined the prospecting process as moving leads from above the FUNNEL down to the top of the FUNNEL, where they become prospects. Prospects should move into the top of the FUNNEL only when the new prospect criteria have been satisfied. This diligent approach prevents salespeople from sinking time into such tasks as "demo given" or "proposal submitted" before they know that the lead has become a valid prospect. When a lead has passed the new prospect criteria, it's clearly a prospect worth pursuing. The

> Use your new prospect criteria to convert leads into prospects

firm should now feel comfortable expending company resources on it.

New Prospect Criteria	Status
Review website or research the company	√
Credit check confirmed	√
Payment history satisfactory	√
Financially strong (balance sheet)	√
Face-to-face meeting	
NDA signed	√
Sense of urgency	√
Verifies a possible fit	
Technical expertise available	
Local decision making	

Figure 9 Suggested New Prospect Criteria

Make the first prospecting call a face-to-face meeting

Why research a company before your first meeting? So you avoid asking questions like "What are your products?" Your contact wants to sense that you have done your homework.

If you're targeting smaller companies, conduct credit checks or ascertain their payment history first to save a lot of grief. If the firm's credit rating doesn't meet your company's standard, you might decide not to make the prospecting call.

It may require more than one face-to-face meeting and involve more than one contact to determine when a prospect has passed the new prospect criteria, especially where large accounts are involved. One face-to-face meeting typically accomplishes the job in small to mid-size companies. Occasionally, you will uncover other leads during your prospecting meetings. This alone can justify the expense of flying somewhere to engage in first face-to-face prospecting calls. Not only are they key to helping you convert the lead into a prospect; they also build rapport, helping you see nuances and other non-verbal communications.

It's a good idea to sign a non-disclosure agreement (NDA) at the beginning of a first prospecting call, to help the lead feel more comfortable sharing information with you. Either ask if they have a NDA you could sign, or take your own company's version, developed to protect the interests of both parties, and offer it when the lead has none of its own.

Many companies include the lead's sense of urgency as a valid new prospect criterion, without which it could take years to close the sale. If the buyer's time frame exceeds your normal sales cycle, they obviously don't pass the sense of urgency criterion, and so should remain a lead. Saving these abandoned leads to a file for reviewing is wise; they're clearly another source of future leads. (Who knows? Something dynamic may happen that increases the sense of urgency.)

If your customers require in-house technical expertise to use your products include "technical expertise available" in your new prospect criteria.

"Funding available" is better suited to Phase 1 of the FUNNEL (Sales Criteria), because more than one meeting is usually needed to develop a trusting business relationship, one in which the prospect will be prepared to share financial information. That level of trust is unlikely to exist during prospecting calls, especially those made by phone. That's why "funding available" is not a new prospect criteria.

When assigned a new sales territory with no leads and no prospects, consider loading the top of your FUNNEL with at least six new prospects before deciding which one to pursue. When it comes to a sense of urgency, your fifth or sixth prospect might be a better fit than your first.

In her first year selling to corporations, Kim had only two prospects in the top of her FUNNEL. She focused exclusively on one of them and, after three months, closed her first order. She'll never forget the excitement of coming back to the office and getting all those hugs. She then focused on her second prospect, and closed its order three months later. Now her FUNNEL was empty. A few days after the second sale closed, this woman's competitor – someone who had worked both these accounts – asked if she would share over lunch how she won the orders. He had been the top sales professional in his company the previous year. Towards the end of lunch he said, "Kim, the real reason I lost both orders was that I had too many prospects at the bottom of my FUNNEL. I didn't have enough time to devote to those two prospects." Kim blanched. Where would she have been had she lost both of these orders? She'd have had an empty FUNNEL and the daunting task of restarting her prospecting program from scratch six months into her efforts! She learned two important lessons from this discussion: not to spend most of her time on closing the first prospect that enters her FUNNEL, and to manage the number of prospects in the bottom of the FUNNEL.

Don't spend too much time qualifying leads. They either satisfy your new prospect criteria or they don't. If they don't, consider abandoning them after a couple of prospecting calls, and pursue leads that do pass the new prospect criteria.

Once you've defined your new prospect criteria, determine whether your existing leads and prospects retain that status. Existing prospects that don't pass the new prospect criteria revert to leads. Existing leads that don't pass all the new prospect criteria also remain leads.

Summary

- Each company's new prospect criteria is unique.
- It is developed by the FUNNEL design team or sales management.
- Sales management and key sales professionals must be involved in its design.

- In small companies, the president or CEO should be part of the design team.

- Utilize your company's new prospect criteria to qualify new prospects.

- Include the "face-to-face meeting" criterion in your new prospect criteria.

- Face-to-face meetings make it easier to get answers to the new prospect criteria.

- The entire sales force must use the same new prospect criteria.

- The FUNNEL design team or sales management updates new prospect criteria.

- Get the new prospect criteria design right to avoid grief later.

14. Target a Senior Executive

There are four principal reasons why you want to target a Senior Executive on the first prospecting call.

Determining the Corporate Pain

Senior Executives play a key role in the decision-making process. They know where pain exists in their organizations; they often lose sleep thinking about it. Corporate pain can be found in the answers to such questions as:

"What are the major obstacles you expect to encounter in the next two years?"

"Where are you looking to improve your productivity?"

"How are you planning to go global?"

Feel free to customize your own list of questions to determine your prospect's corporate pain.

Identifying the Approver

Look for the Senior Executive in your prospect's organization who serves as the approver, the one with the final approving authority to purchase or lease your products. There is only one approver per prospect. Unfortunately, the approver also has the discretionary ability to spend these funds on other projects or initiatives. By meeting a Senior Executive on your first prospecting call, you increase your chances that this person is either the approver, or someone in a position to identify the approver to you.

Don't Get Level Locked

Win those first appointments with Senior Executives and you avoid getting level locked, a situation brought on by making too many of your early prospecting and sales calls on the same low- or mid-level managers who tell you not to call on a Senior Executive. It happens to all sales professionals, so just aim to minimize its occurrence.

Towards the end of your meeting, if the call is going well, ask:

"Based on this conversation, Mr. Smith, who else in your company should I meet?"

If you are given a name, ask:

"Would you mind informing Ms. Green of our meeting, and that I will be contacting her next week?"

If, during this first meeting, one or more names are dropped, make note of them. If a particular name comes up several times, you might ask:

"What is Ms. Green's position in the company and what role would she play if our discussions were to go further?"

Allows Ongoing Access

Develop rapport with Senior Executives to give you easier access to this resource when and if it's needed later in the sales cycle.

When a well established multinational first entered the computer business, it targeted the education market from elementary schools to universities.

At an education trade show, a senior government bureaucrat responsible for education visited the booth. Kim, a sales professional, quickly established rapport with him during a demonstration of the company's educational software.

They had coffee after the show, and he encouraged her to phone if she ever ran into trouble selling to educational institutions. Kim decided to maintain contact with this senior bureaucrat, dropping him a short note to inform him whenever a school district, community college, or university ordered a computer system from her, even including a brief description of the application. Several years later, after a post secondary institution issued a tender for a large instructional computer system, and after the RFP closed, the selection committee decided to change the specifications to favor another vendor. Kim, who had of course spent months with her own systems people working on the proposal, decided to inform the senior bureaucrat of the situation. He immediately phoned the principal of the college, who advised the selection committee to abide by their original specifications. The result: Kim's company won a $300,000 order.

15. The Six-Step Prospecting Process

This six-step prospecting process assists sales professionals in planning and executing that first important prospecting call. Prospecting begins by obtaining the interview.

STEP 1: Obtaining the First Appointment

Most sales professionals agree it's very difficult to obtain a first appointment with a Senior Executive. It requires focusing all your knowledge, skill, and practice. However, once you're in, there is a great sense of satisfaction. Even after several years of obtaining high-level appointments, I was pleased with a hit rate of 50%. But now, I've developed a new approach that has taken my success rate to over 80%. I refer to it as empowering the screening source, and it is one of four different approaches used to obtain a first appointment.

- Traditional

- Empowering the screening source

- Referral from another company or person

- Referral by a lobbyist

Prospecting is hard work, but the payoff is enormous. Before we discuss these four approaches, let's review some phone tips.

Phone Call, Voice Mail or E-mail

> **Don't leave a voice mail when trying to obtain a first interview**

What's the optimal method for obtaining your first meeting? The phone. If the Executive Assistant or Senior Executive doesn't answer the phone, don't leave a voice mail. Call back every day, never leaving a message, until you finally make contact. Otherwise, you may get pegged as a nuisance. People are so busy today that they don't have time to return calls, particularly to strangers. How many people will answer an e-mail requesting a first appointment with somebody they don't know? Correct: close to zero.

After a first meeting, e-mail messages are more effective than phone calls, and responses much faster. If you do use the phone to contact prospects for subsequent calls, leave a voice mail only once. Include in your voice mail a brief outline of what you wish to discuss. Everyone has a preferred method of communication. Determine what it is for each of your prospects by asking them. One client asked not to be contacted by e-mail, as he gets so many that he can't possibly read them all. He asked to be contacted by phone and leave a return phone number, to make it easier for him to return calls.

Ask a number of questions through e-mail, and chances are, only the first question gets answered.

To combat this, some people number the questions and leave several blank lines under each question. But the best method for getting the answers to multiple questions is to ask one question per e-mail. If you have four questions to ask, send four e-mails spread over a few days.

Make Appointments to Fit Planning Window

Begin by giving some thought to the Senior Executive's planning window and looking at your own schedule to see how many days or weeks you are fully booked. Typically, the higher the person's position, the longer period of time they are booked, so if you're not free for a week, you can guess that he or she may be tied up for two weeks. By anticipating your prospect's planning window when you call to make that first appointment, you exhibit a respect that will help in clinching the appointment. As you get to know your prospects better, ask them how far in advance they are typically booked.

> **Anticipate the Senior Executive's planning window**

Phones Are for Making Appointments

Shortly after his transfer to Seattle, Dana was given the remote territories of Alaska and eastern Washington State. At the time, his company had no customers in these territories, but every month the entire sales force would receive a number of leads from head office.

> **It is a mistake to save time by qualifying leads on the phone**

While reviewing these leads, Dana discovered one from a small university located in Southeast Washington State. When he phoned, staff informed him that they had an old model of one of his company's printers and it was not working. Dana obtained permission to meet with them the following week to discuss the problem. During this meeting with their computer committee, Dana determined that a $5 part of their printer – obsolete for five years – needed replacement. He offered to take the defective part back to Seattle to see if his service organization could help, after which the university inquired if Dana's company had a computer system that might meet their current requirements, one that would replace a version installed by Dana's firm's competitor. Three trips later, over a period of two months, Dana netted a $180,000 sale. (Incidentally, his service manager was also able to replace the $5 part.) Shortly after the computer's installation, Dana's new client mentioned a university ten miles away that might be interested in a similar system. Five visits to this new university over the course of three months resulted in another sale, this time for $350,000.

Had this sales professional attempted to qualify the first university on the phone, it is unlikely he would have won either of these sales. It is a mistake to save time by qualifying leads on the phone. When prospecting, use the phone only to obtain that very important first face-to-face meeting.

Duration of Prospecting Call

Ask for half-hour meetings when making appointments

In today's business climate, Senior Executives are so busy that they'll rarely give a sales professional more than half an hour for a first prospecting call, especially if the two live in the same city. It is unwise to request more than that. After your lead has agreed to a meeting, suggest a time and date that fits in the planning window, while having alternate times and dates available.

If you are traveling a great distance to make this call (say, Seattle to Denver), you can ask for an hour, or maybe even more. If you're traveling from Seattle to Asia, you can even push for a three-hour meeting.

Traditional

The traditional approach is to phone the Senior Executive for a first appointment. More often than not, you'll end up talking to the Executive Assistant, who serves as an excellent screening source. Most sales professionals pursuing this traditional approach will be lucky to achieve hit rates of 50%. Obtaining a first interview in this fashion is not easy.

Sales professionals should make the call themselves for two reasons:

- Scoring a first meeting requires the skills of a seasoned sales professional. Less experienced individuals will likely lose the opportunity.

- It allows for establishing initial rapport with the screening source or Senior Executive.

> **Sales professionals should obtain the first interview by themselves**

Salespersons' horror stories of being unable to obtain a first appointment with a Senior Executive point to an Executive Assistant's skill at screening them out.

But top sales professionals will research a company before they make the phone call, and it won't take long for the Senior Executive or his/her screener to determine that the sales professional has done his homework – learned about the company, its markets, and its products. While such background information has been available traditionally from annual reports, K1s, newspapers, magazines, and business directories, today, the majority of companies offer it on their own websites, which any savvy sales person will have scanned before phoning. Still, since many websites do not contain the names of Senior Executives, it is wise to research business directories as well. Sometimes a president's or executive's name is mentioned in press releases on the website. You should also focus on determining who the prospective company's strategic partners are, and their roles. Plan no more than a two-minute phone call, as your objective is to obtain an interview, not to sell.

Once you have armed yourself with information on the company, including the names of its Senior Executives, and dialed the number, there is still one more hurdle: Executive Assistants who screen calls. Never underestimate their power and

> **Develop a personal business relationship with the Executive Assistant**

influence. Not only do they control access to the Senior Executives; in today's business culture, they can be invaluable. Your mission is to empower them to become one of your advocates.

First, phone the company's receptionist to obtain the name of the Executive Assistant.

"Do you mind telling me the name of Ms. Green's Executive Assistant?"

Receptionist: "It's Ted Brown. Would you like me to connect you?"

Now, when the Executive Assistant answers your call, you are able to address him or her by name.

If you are unable to obtain the Executive Assistant's name, listen for it as soon as you are connected. Write it down and use it several times during the conversation. If the individual doesn't offer his name, ask for it. Doesn't it make *you* feel good when someone uses your name during conversation?

Five methods to determine a Senior Executive's name:

• Ask the receptionist

• Check company's website

• Investigate business directories

• Review newspapers or magazine articles

• Pursue a referral

Constantly scan newspapers, appropriate magazines, and other publications, watching for articles about prospective customers. You are looking for a valid business reason why the Senior Executive would want to meet with you.

Call Senior Executives before 8:00 am and after 6:00 pm

Some sales professionals call after hours to obtain the name of an Executive Assistant or Senior Executive through the company's voice mail system. Better yet, call the Senior Executive's office before 8:00 am or after 6:00 pm, and you'll be surprised how often you find the Senior Executive answering the phone directly.

For future reference, place the name of the Executive Assistant on the top left-hand corner, and the Senior Executive's partner's name on the top right-hand corner of the Senior Executive's business card. This makes it easier to remember their names on subsequent phone calls or meetings.

Making the first phone call involves three steps:

- State your name, title, and company's name.

- Ask to speak to the Senior Executive by name.

- If screened, state that you would appreciate a half-hour meeting with that executive.

"Mr. Brown, this is Tony Smith. How are you today? I am the Regional Sales Manager with Company X and I've had lots of success lately with helping companies like yours. Our solutions are quite popular in the marketplace, and I expect Ms. Green is aware of us. My purpose is to talk to her for a few moments to strike a possible relationship. I need only three minutes with her on the phone."

Here is where the trouble starts. Generally speaking, the longer you talk, the more difficult it is to obtain the interview, as you increase your chances of giving the wrong answer to one of the screening questions. You don't have advance warning as to what these questions will be. Executive Assistants are trained to screen out salespeople and they are very good at it. As soon as you are asked for the purpose of the proposed meeting, be prepared to make a short statement similar to the one quoted above, but customize it to fit your style and situation.

The longer you speak, the more difficult it is to obtain the appointment

If you are put through to the Senior Executive, remember that your only objective is to obtain an interview. Here's an example of one very successful sales manager who trained his sales team to use the "value proposition" to obtain an appointment.

"Ms. Green, Mardon provides full IT solutions in your industry – we have won several recent sales campaigns with businesses like yours – for the simple reason that we save you significant costs, are more reliable in the long-run, and can de-risk the project implementation. I have references to prove it! Would you like an alternative to your present supplier, or a more cost-effective solution?"

If the reply is affirmative, the sales professional might say:

"Could we have a half hour meeting at 10:00 in the morning on Tuesday, March 25?"

Don't put the onus on the lead to return your call

Remember to keep in mind what you've guessed to be the Senior Executive's planning window when asking this question. Have an alternative time and date available as back-up, should the first date not be convenient. Once the appointment is confirmed, thank the Senior Executive and get off the phone. Never put the onus on the Executive Assistant or Senior Executive to return your call. Why should they want to call you, an unknown person, when they are so busy that they barely have time to return calls to people they already know?

The biggest mistake salespeople make during the prospecting process is attempting to qualify the prospective customer during this first phone call. Use the phone only to obtain the appointment. Do your qualifying face to face. As companies downsize, the ranks of Executive Assistants are thinning out, replaced in part by voice mail, which has made it even more difficult for sales professionals to contact Senior Executives. Don't leave a message when you are connected by voice mail. A busy executive won't take time to call you back. If you do leave a voice mail and don't receive a reply for several days, resist the desire to call again. As mentioned earlier, a second message will brand you as a nuisance. It is best to keep phoning without leaving voice mail until you make contact.

To maximize your information-gathering efforts on the corporate pain and names of contacts in the organization, try to ensure that only you and the Senior Executive will be present at this first interview. To ascertain if this will be the scenario, ask the Senior Executive or the Executive Assistant if anyone else will attend the meeting. Should you learn that the chief technology officer will join you, consider bringing your own technical resource.

> The best information comes when only you and the Senior Executive are present

Empowering the Screening Source

This approach results in success rates of over 80% for obtaining that important first interview, because it empowers the screening source. The traditional approach views the screening source as a potential obstacle, and looks for ways to get around him or her. Given that Senior Executives often take their Executive Assistants with them to a new job or company, the Executive Assistant becomes well versed as to who gets to meet the boss. Empowering the screening source involves four steps.

i. Write one or two short paragraphs stating the objective of the meeting. Include one valid reason why the Senior Executive would wish to meet with you. This is not a form letter; it needs to be tailored to the person you wish to meet. It is not an easy task to write this short letter. You need to put yourself in the position of the Senior Executive, asking: "What's in it for me?" Ensure "what is in it" will positively impact the screening source.

> Write a short letter explaining why the Senior Executive should agree to the meeting

Here's what someone in the business of helping companies going global in Asia, might say.

"I enjoyed reading about your company in yesterday's Chronicle and note that you are planning to expand your operations into Asia. We are in the business of assisting companies expanding into global markets. A number of our clients will attest to how we have assisted them. I would appreciate a half-hour meeting with you to learn more about your expansion plans. At the end of this meeting, I'll have more insight as to whether we can be of value to you. Then you will know if you would like to continue the discussions."

Empower the screening source with the decision to take your request to the Senior Executive

ii. Determine the name of the screening source and the Senior Executive prior to your phone call. Techniques for doing this were discussed in the traditional approach.

iii. Phone the Senior Executive for the appointment, knowing there is a 90%+ chance that the Executive Assistant will answer the phone. You are going to say something like this:

"Mr. Brown, this is Tony Smith of the ABC Company. How are you today?"

"Just fine, and feel free to call me Ron."

"Ron, I would appreciate having a half-hour appointment with Ms. Green. May I send you a very short letter outlining the purpose of the meeting?"

"Sure, go ahead and send it, Tony."

"May I send it by e-mail?"

When he agrees, ask if it can be sent as an attachment to the e-mail, as many people will not open unknown attachments, and a formatted Word document looks more professional when printed and presented to the Senior Executive. You would then say:

"Ron, after you've read the attachment, if you think that Ms. Green would benefit from this meeting, do you mind setting up an appointment?"

This is the empowering statement; you're assigning the decision to the screening source.

iv. Call the Executive Assistant the next day to confirm he received the e-mail and could open the attachment. By letting the Executive

Assistant make the decision whether or when to schedule the meeting, you have empowered the screening source. One of the following four scenarios will likely occur:

- The Senior Executive will agree to meet with you.

- The Senior Executive will not meet with you (unlikely if you've written a compelling letter).

- The Executive Assistant will make the decision and get back to you with the time and date for the meeting (not as rare as you might think).

- The Executive Assistant will screen you out (rarely in my experience if you use this approach).

In addition to mailing a thank you letter to the Senior Executive, also e-mail a separate thank you note to the Executive Assistant after the interview.

Send a thank you note to the screening source once you've had the interview

On a first phone call to the Senior Executive, designed solely to request an appointment, the Executive Assistant is likely to ask:

"What is the purpose of the meeting?"

By giving the screening source the opportunity to ask this question, you risk not knowing the direction the questioning will go and what answers will be acceptable to win the appointment.

Your success rate will be much higher if you pre-empt this questioning, and obtain agreement to e-mail a one-paragraph letter articulating the purpose of the appointment. The only difference between this and the traditional approach is the way in which the reason behind the meeting is communicated. In this approach, the reason is given in a well thought-out document, whereas in the traditional approach, the reason is given on the phone. If the Senior Executive answers the phone, however, opt for the traditional approach.

Referral

The referral is the most effective way to obtain an interview

Although this is the most effective approach to obtaining an interview with a prospective customer, it works only when you or another person in your company know one of your customers, who, in turn knows a Senior Executive in the lead's organization. When this referral either gives you permission to use his name, or introduces you to the Senior Executive, you have an excellent chance of obtaining the interview.

Use like-ranked customers to introduce you to like-ranked prospects

Sales professionals should watch for the opportunity to link like-ranked executives from their customer organizations to like-ranked executives in targeted companies. If you work for a large company, find such linkage by broadcasting an inquiry to your senior management, asking if anyone knows a Senior Executive in the targeted company.

Lobbyist

Another approach is contracting lobbyists – particularly useful if you require a meeting with a ranking bureaucrat in a government agency or with a Senior Executive of a Fortune 1000 company. Consultants working in lobbyist firms often have close personal relationships with senior bureaucrats, influential politicians, and Senior Executives. It could take you six months to obtain interviews that a lobbyist can swing in six weeks. And lobbyists can arrange appointments you cannot obtain by yourself. The downside to this approach is its expense, but if the potential business is significant, the expense may be worthwhile.

STEP 2: Preparing the Call

Here are tips for preparing the call:

Schedule Calls Every Two Hours

If you can get from one call to another within half an hour, schedule prospecting calls about every two hours. That way, should your call end up lasting one hour, you will still have ten minutes to write your call report, thirty minutes to get to your next appointment, and ten minutes to allow for heavy traffic – and you will still arrive ten minutes before your next meeting. If you don't schedule your time this way, you will find yourself nervous during the latter part of your meetings in anticipation of being late for your next appointment. As soon as you look at your watch, the person with whom you are meeting will sense that you are more interested in getting to your next appointment than dealing with him. Some salespeople place their wrist watches on the table to avoid looking at their wrist.

> **Don't schedule your prospecting calls too close together**

Breakfast and Dinner Meetings

If you find your prospect is busy during working hours, suggest a breakfast meeting. This worked for me when a Senior Executive was booked for several months. When I suggested a breakfast meeting, he jumped at the opportunity and stated:

> "What a wonderful idea! No one else has ever suggested that to me."

If you are selling into Asia, dinner meetings are very popular, and they save you worry about getting through your agenda in a half hour. Dinner meetings can go on for hours, giving you lots of time to develop rapport. One caution: In Asia, you should wait for the Senior Executive to initiate the business part of the meeting. If they don't, they are not ready to discuss the business issues. They want to get to know you better. In this case, schedule a second meeting before you leave the country.

The Four- or Five-Call Prospecting Day

One way to get proficient at making prospecting calls is to pick a prospecting day two or three times a month, and make four or five calls those days. Those who don't enjoy prospecting should consider making several joint prospecting calls with other sales professionals who are really good at it. The more calls you make, the more proficient you will become, and the more you will enjoy making them.

No Calls Without an Appointment

Some sales professionals define cold calls as dropping in on a potential client without an appointment. This is not recommended. Other sales professionals define cold calls as the first call by phone. If you are selling products valued at more than about $25,000, use this first phone call only to make a face-to-face appointment. Sometimes, when you are making prospecting calls in a large office building, it is tempting to drop in on another company whose name is on your suspect list. If you act on this urge, I recommend that you restrict yourself to asking the receptionist there for the name of the appropriate person or their business card for later contact. Speaking to the receptionist and not the Senior Executive, does not rank as a cold call.

Research Your Targeted Industries

Before you make that first call, research not just the company but its industry as well. A good source for this information is trade magazines found in central libraries.

Car Route and Parking in a Strange City

Let's say you've just flown into a city for the first time late on a Sunday afternoon to make prospecting calls over the next few days. Your first meeting is at 8:30 am downtown on Monday, and you are driving from outside the downtown core.

You have no idea of morning rush hour traffic patterns, the number of one-way streets, or where to locate convenient parking. Drive to your first meeting's location on the Sunday evening so you can sort this out. And be sure to pack your cell phone and contact's number the next morning, in case you encounter an unavoidable delay.

Check Supply of Business Cards

You want to check your supply of business cards regularly. Nothing is more embarrassing than being unable to exchange a business card, especially during a prospecting call. This does not make a good first impression and becomes a major problem if you discover a shortage during out-of-town business trips, so keep extras on hand. To ensure you don't run out, keep your business cards in the following places:

Keep extra business cards handy

- business card holder

- wallet or purse

- briefcase

- computer or notebook case

- glove compartment

- boat

- golf bag

- partner's wallet or purse

- gym bag

If you carry some of your partner's cards and the two of you are out of town together, it can save the day. People usually exchange business cards when you offer yours. If they don't, make a point of politely requesting it. If they don't have one handy, ask for their e-mail address and write it on one of your business cards. I wouldn't ask them to mail it to you, because some people, meeting you for the first time, may either forget or take exception to your request.

Prospecting Call Agenda

Using agendas for your prospecting calls not only assists you in staying organized, but also offers a better first impression to the Senior Executive. Remember to place the agenda on your company's first page letterhead, as this makes it easier for the person to contact you (Figure 10).

Before you start the business part of your meeting, state the reason why the Senior Executive agreed to meet with you in the first place. List this reason as the first item on your agenda.

Mardon Marketing Company Inc.

ABC Company Inc.
Betty Green
President

April 30, 200X

- Reason for meeting
- Background of ABC
- Business outlook
- Strategic objectives
- Obstacles encountered
- New markets & distribution methods
- Strategic relationships
- Overview of Mardon Marketing
- Next steps
-

31X Cordova Drive • Seattle, WA 9800X • Phone: (206) 656-001X • Fax: (206) 656-002X
openshow@keepingthefunnelfull.com   www.keepingthefunnelfull.com

Figure 10 Sample Agenda – Prospecting Call

List of Questions for Prospecting Call

Early in my sales career, I was driving across a metropolitan city one day after making a prospecting call, when I realized I had forgotten to ask two key questions. Devastated, I vowed this would never happen again.

Have you ever been in a similar position, wondering whether one of those unanswered questions would qualify the company to become a prospect? Unfortunately, it is not professional to phone back to ask forgotten questions. Arming yourself with a list of questions makes it difficult to forget key queries and the order in which they should be asked. It also forces you to think through what you wish to accomplish on the call.

> Develop a generic list of questions for the first prospecting call

Use your list of questions for all your first prospecting calls. If you are part of a sales team or a sales district, develop the list together; it will benefit each sales professional and serve as a great brainstorming exercise, collecting your and your colleagues' best ideas. Competent sales professionals focus only on questions about the prospective customer's needs while listening for a product fit. Don't bring up the topic of products on this first call unless asked. Where major sales are at stake, invest in several meetings with different people until you understand the corporate pain. At that point, you have earned the right to request a product presentation in the context of their needs.

Reserve a one-inch space below each question so that you can scribble cryptic comments or notations to indicate that the question was answered, and to remind you of the exchange. Aim to have no blank spaces under the questions by the end of your meeting. Finally, place this list of questions inside the front cover of your hard-copy notebook to make it unobtrusive, as it is for your eyes only.

The sample list of questions for a first call on Betty Green is shown in Figure 11.

ABC Company Inc.
Betty Green

April 30, 200X

- Tell me the background of the ABC Company.

- What is the outlook for your business in the next two years?

- What do you view as the major factors for your company's success?

- What are the major obstacles you expect over the next year?

- What do you want to accomplish during your next fiscal year?
  - What is your fiscal year?

- Where do you see your new markets?

- What has been your experience with expanding your product lines?
  - What worked?   - What didn't work?

- Is there someone else in your company I should meet?

- May I give you a brief overview of my company?

- Let's briefly review the next steps we have agreed to take.

Figure 11 Sample List of Questions – Prospecting Call

STEP 3: Qualifying Face to Face
Prospecting Call Objective

All prospecting calls have the same objective:

To verify if ABC Company is a good fit and would benefit from your product.

Call on a Senior Executive

The best way to identify the pain is to qualify face-to-face with a Senior Executive. Unfortunately, it is not always possible to secure a first prospecting call with a Senior Executive, but competent sales professionals get very good at it. Meeting with the

Senior Executive may identify more than one prospect, while calls on lower levels of management usually identify only one.

Introducing the Agenda

Introducing the agenda is a great way to transition to the business part of the meeting (Figure 12). It should take between 15 and 20 seconds. Here's an example of such a conversation:

"Ms. Green, I appreciate your offer to spend half an hour with me this morning, and I intend to make our meeting worthwhile for you."

"It's nice to meet you, Tony. Call me Betty."

"Thank you, Betty. It was quite a traffic problem getting over here, I had no idea it was so bad."

"I know. It gets worse every year. Won't you come and sit down?"

Breaking the Ice

• Weather
• Traffic problems
• Introductory banter

↓

(Transition)

↓

Business Part

• Discuss the reason for the call
• Introduce agenda
• Tacit permission to take notes

Figure 12 Introducing the Agenda

This is a signal that Betty wants to get to the business part of the meeting as soon as possible. There is no reason to continue breaking the ice; doing so may annoy her.

"Thank you, Betty. I've prepared an agenda. May I introduce it to you?"

"Sure."

"By the way, I've looked at your website, which is very nicely done. What I'd like to accomplish today is understand ABC's background and your strategic objectives. This will help me see if I can assist you in realizing these objectives."

"Tony, right now one of our problems is expanding into Asia."

"We certainly have expertise in helping companies establish themselves in Asia. I'd appreciate it if you would share how you are presently marketing your products. Then I'll take two or three minutes to present an overview of what we do. After that, we can determine if it makes sense for us to continue discussions at a later date. Does that sound okay for our agenda?"

"Tony, that sounds like a good plan."

"Betty, I'd like to add another agenda item called 'Going Global in Asia.' Will that be okay?"

"Sure."

"Do you wish to add any additional topics to our agenda?"

"No thanks, Tony."

Ask if there is another topic to be added to the agenda

Since Betty has given you the go-ahead on another topic, place "Going Global in Asia" beside the blank bullet at the bottom of both copies of the agenda. Now you start the business part of the meeting beginning with her new topic.

As you begin the interview, open your notebook. Voila! There is your list of questions on the inside front cover to help keep you on track. As a courtesy, many sales professionals will obtain tacit approval from the Senior Executive to take notes. Taking notes without their permission makes some people nervous, and they may become less communicative. Betty doesn't need to know that you are working from a list of questions.

When you are making this call, Betty will sometimes point you to other persons in her organization and may even introduce you to them. If this doesn't happen, consider requesting an introduction. In any event, you will want to meet them later. You may be pleasantly surprised by how friendly and helpful lower levels of management will become after Betty introduces you. Unless they ask, however, you have no reason to explain your relationship with Betty.

Be certain to honor the time commitment. When the half hour is up, you might say:

"Betty, I am enjoying this meeting to learn about your major issues. I note that our half hour is up. But I have more time if you do."

If the meeting has gone well and she has the time, you can usually extend your meeting another fifteen minutes. If you are lucky, you will get another half hour. In these extended scenarios, the lead gets to call when the meeting is over. Based on my experience, the optimal time for this first call seems to be about forty-five minutes. I am delighted when awarded this extension. Allow the other person to do 75% or more of the talking. After all, it's a fact-finding mission.

> **Allow the other person to do 75% of the talking**

You'll know you have answers to all your questions when there are no blank spaces beneath each question towards the end of the meeting. Thank the person for agreeing to meet with you.

Level Locked

One pitfall sales professionals encounter is getting level locked with a low-level manager. When your first three or four calls are all with this manager, you may find that you have lost your ability to move upward in the organization. Try asking this manager:

"Do you mind introducing me to Ms. Green?"

"Tony, there is no need for you to talk to anyone else. I will represent you to her if that becomes necessary."

You are now level locked, and this almost always results in a longer sales cycle and sometimes in losing the sale. Not good news!

Another approach might be to suggest:

"When it is appropriate, perhaps I could give a short presentation to Ms. Green and yourself?"

Everyone gets level locked sometime, and there is no sure way out. The best solution is to call high in the first place, even if it means waiting for the right opportunity to be introduced.

STEP 4: Handling the Good Fit

Describe how your solutions have helped similar companies

As you obtain answers to your list of questions, you should be determining the nature of the corporate pain and listening for names being dropped. Watch for parallels between the company that you are calling on and your other customers. Sometimes this analogy affords you the opportunity to describe how your solutions have resolved similar problems with other clients. If the lead shows interest, you might ask if they would like to meet their counterpart in your customer's organization. Do not shorten the dialogue when the person is taking a long time answering your questions. This means you should stay with the question and invoke onion-peeling techniques. You may hear answers to later questions. Don't forget to listen for names to be dropped, and consider that an opportunity to ask if this is someone you should meet. If the lead passes the new prospect criteria, you will have a good fit.

If the lead appears interested in extending the discussion around the current question, you may not get all your other questions answered. If this happens, either ask for more time, or schedule another appointment to finish the agenda.

You should:

- Verify they have passed the new prospect criteria

- Obtain agreement for next steps to be taken by both parties

- Determine names of others to involve later

- Ask if they are using consultants

- Determine the consultant's name, company name, and specific role

- Identify the competition

Include a brief overview of your company toward the end of the agenda, but present your products only if asked. You can leave a copy of your corporate brochure at the end of the interview, but it's even more effective to include selected corporate literature with your thank you letter. Ask for copies of their corporate and product brochures. Sometime during this meeting, let them know that you have viewed their website.

> A fit occurs when the lead passes the new prospect criteria

If you don't have time to establish that the lead passes the new prospect criteria, you should schedule additional meetings with either the person you are calling on, or someone else in the organization. Until you obtain the right answers to all the new prospect criteria, don't move this prospect into the top of your FUNNEL. End the interview with thanks, and summarize the next steps both parties have agreed to take.

STEP 5: Handling the Bad Fit

If after about fifteen minutes you are getting far too many wrong answers – such as "We have no budget for new capital expenditures this fiscal year" – explain that although there may not be a fit now, there may be one in the future. Ask if they would like to be placed on your corporate mailing list to receive periodic information about your company, its products, and customer profiles.

If the lead doesn't
pass the new prospect
criteria, lose early

If you have developed a good rapport, don't hesitate to ask if they know of any other companies that might be interested in meeting with you. It is important to leave this call as soon as possible, because you are wasting their time and yours. Bring the interview to a close at the first appropriate opportunity and thank them for their time.

If the lead doesn't pass your new prospect criteria, lose early. A bad fit can take an inexhaustible amount of your time. I've seen some companies spend two years calling on bad fits to no avail.

There are hundreds of other leads sitting above your FUNNEL that will give you better answers to your list of questions. If you have extra time before your next call, why not make other appointments, taking into account the Senior Executives' planning window?

STEP 6: Reviewing the Call

Reviewing the call is the last step. Complete the call report as soon as you leave the interview, because your recall of the points discussed will decrease exponentially with time. You'll start forgetting key points even as you go down the elevator. Not only that, but you might forget the meaning of some of those cryptic notes on your list of questions.

Complete the call report
immediately after the
interview

The best place to write the call report – a five-to-ten-minute job – is near where the interview was conducted, such as in the building's lobby or coffee shop, or in your car. I've found it useful to download my call report template from my laptop. A wireless laptop allows you to transmit the call report right away, if any of the information is time critical.

If you are running short of time, capture the call

report on your pocket recorder as you are driving to your next meeting. Then transfer it quickly to your computer at the end of the day. Just remember to capture the information in some fashion within minutes of the call. The longer you wait, the more key information you will forget. Follow up with a short thank you message either by e-mail or letter, including a short paragraph reviewing what actions both parties agreed to take. The thank you letter is more effective than an e-mail message.

> **Send a thank you letter immediately following the interview**

16. Key Points for Making an Effective Prospecting Call

Before the Interview:

- Listen and search constantly for names of Senior Executives in your targeted companies.

- Use the phone only to make the appointment. Don't leave messages or you'll be labeled a pest.

- Have a valid business reason why the Senior Executive should agree to meet with you.

- Use the 'empowering the screening source' approach to obtain the interview.

- If in the same city, ask for a half-hour meeting; if traveling to another city, ask for an hour.

- Allow two hours between the start of one call and the start of the next.

- Create a written agenda and list of questions applicable to all first prospecting calls.

During the Interview:

- Arrive at your meeting ten to fifteen minutes early and meet the Executive Assistant.

- Thank the Executive Assistant for his or her time and offer your business card.

- This is a fact-finding mission. You are there to get all the answers to your new prospect criteria.

- Exchange business cards with the Senior Executive.

- Start the business portion of the meeting by introducing the agenda (15 to 20 seconds).

- In a low-key manner, obtain permission to take notes.

- When you open your notebook, the list of questions should appear inside the left-hand front cover.

- Address the valid business reason why the Senior Executive agreed to meet with you.

- Execute the meeting by following the agenda and the list of questions.

- Record cryptic comments and names dropped, in the blank spaces beneath each question.

- Remember to ask the remaining questions (those with blank spaces) before end of the meeting.

- Show interest by maintaining eye contact for as much of the meeting as possible.

- Obtain agreement on future action items for both yourself and your new prospect.

- Thank the person at the end of the meeting.

After the Interview:

- Capture the information on your call report as soon as possible (within 5 to 10 minutes).

- Send a thank you letter and confirm the actions agreed to by both parties.

- When the prospect knows you understand the firm's needs, you have earned the right to ask for a product presentation.

Notes

Notes

PART 3:
THE SELLING PROCESS

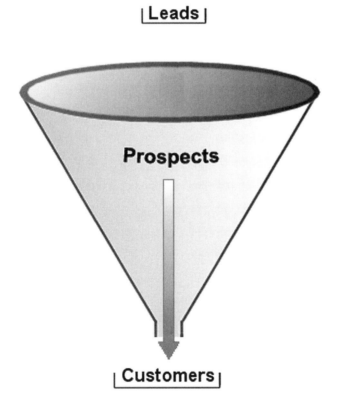

17. Solution Selling

The Successful Sales Professional

Solution selling involves determining the needs of a prospect before pitching your product. Once you know these needs, you are in a position to deliver presentations and submit the proposal in the context of the prospect's needs. It's all about being customer centered rather than product centered. The prospect will recognize that you are more interested in offering a solution than in selling a product. Far too many salespeople pitch their products without a clue about their prospect's needs. These needs arise from the corporate pain of the prospect and the self-interests of each DMP (decision-making process) member.

> Understand your prospect's needs before pitching your products

Corporate Pain

Corporate pain is the obstacle a company must overcome to solve a corporate problem. If you know what keeps the Senior Executive awake at night, you're positioned to determine the corporate pain. Senior Executives see the big picture and can provide a clearer understanding of the corporate pain. Low-level management tends to view corporate pain from within their area of responsibility. When you have developed a rapport with a Senior Executive, you have earned the right to ask the types of questions that will help you uncover the corporate pain.

"What do you see as your major obstacles in achieving next year's revenue target?"

"What are the major challenges to achieving your company's strategic objectives?"

Once the Senior Executive starts discussing the nature of their corporate pain, it is time to be a great listener and stay with the topic.

The more profound your understanding of the prospect's corporate pain, the better positioned you'll be to offer solutions later in your presentations and proposal. Determining the corporate pain is not always an easy task. Presidents of small to mid-sized companies will be the most knowledgeable of the corporate pain, so this is the place to start. If you can't start there, call on another Senior Executive. The smaller the company, the easier it is to obtain that first meeting with the president.

Self-Interest

An equally important consideration to knowing the prospects' pain comes into play in solution selling. This is the concept of self-interest defined by David Hume as "those objective requirements that benefit a person's life." Hume (1711-1776), the Scottish philosopher and economist, perceived the significance of self-interest as a human motivator. In *A Treatise of Human Nature* (1734), he gave his golden rule, "I won't disturb your self-interest if you won't disturb mine." It stands as true today as it did then.

Self-interests are very personal and vary from person to person. Examples of self-interests of the DMP members you are attempting to identify might be:

• A successful implementation of this solution will help my career.

• This solution will shorten my twelve-hour working day.

> DMP members need to know their self-interests will be satisfied

In the context of solution selling, the sales professional and DMP members must each have their self-interests satisfied. The sales professional needs to understand the self-interests of each DMP member, and ensure that each member realizes their self-interests have been satisfied. This must be done subtly. If you don't understand their self-interests, you run the risk of losing the order, even if your solution solves the corporate pain.

It is in the nature of your business relationship and the quality of your listening that you become aware of their self-interests. As your mutual trust increases, DMP members will be more liable to share their personal self-interests.

Selling Hierarchy

Sales professionals fall into one of three levels of a selling hierarchy, differentiated by their ability to determine the prospect's needs (Figure 13). Anyone selling to corporations must be operating at either Level 2 or Level 3.

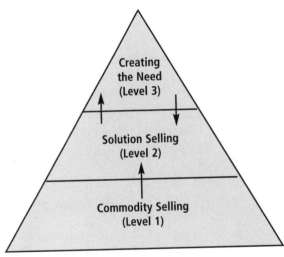

Figure 13 Selling Hierarchy

Level 1 The Commodity Sales Professional

This is the lowest level in selling and is the domain of the commodity sales person. Salespeople operating at this level focus on selling their products, making little or no attempt to determine the prospect's needs. Their modus operandi is getting the sale at whatever price they can. Commodity selling often characterizes retail sales; it is not effective when selling solutions to corporations. If you find yourself delivering a product presentation before you have determined the prospect's needs, you are operating at this level. Break the habit and move up to Level 2.

> Commodity selling doesn't work when selling to corporations

Level 2 Solution Selling

Competent sales professionals focus on determining their prospects' needs before discussing their products. This is the essence of solution selling. These sales professionals know the right questions to ask and are adept at listening for the answers. They know how to drill down through many layers with appropriate questions that uncover the corporate pain. This is referred to as the onion peeling technique. They quickly identify if the sale will be bottoms up, or top down, or both.

Senior Executives are the best source to discover corporate pain

Senior Executives are the best contacts for determining corporate pain, because they see the big picture. They are in a position to make you aware of a number of needs, each pointing to a different prospect. However, as we've established, it is not always possible to call on higher levels of management. Lower-level management may identify needs, but these usually apply to their own departments, and they are not always effective in communicating their needs to Senior Executives. Skillful sales professionals watch for this situation and become adept at conveying lower-level management's needs to Senior Executives without offending the originating source.

Another way to find new prospects is to determine the strategic objectives that support the target firm's corporate vision. That allows you to identify a solution to one or more of their strategic objectives.

In Level 2, sales professionals should:

- call on Senior Executives early in the sales cycle

- determine the corporate vision and strategic objectives

- determine the corporate pain

- understand the self-interests of each DMP member

- win the endorsement of the approver

- offer the best price/performance solution (ROI)

- offer the solution that solves the corporate pain and satisfies all self-interests

- ask for the order

Solution selling is the level that sales professionals must master if they are to be successful in selling to corporations. Sales professionals engaged in solution selling operate at Level 2.

Level 3 Creating the Need

When operating at Level 3, sales professionals understand their prospect's operation in such depth that they uncover needs not yet recognized by anyone in the buying organization. At first glance, this may sound preposterous, but it occasionally happens. Few sales professionals ever get to operate in Level 3, and if they do, it's only transitory.

Stan, a sales professional calling on a multinational corporation, had done an outstanding job identifying needs not yet recognized by its own executive management team. He accomplished this by conducting separate interviews with a number of low-level managers, who provided enough information for him to recognize a significant corporate need. Individually, these managers did not perceive the need because they lacked information from the other low-level managers. Stan brought this corporate need to the attention of the approver, and obtained permission to submit an unsolicited proposal. This resulted in a multi-million dollar contract for a number of large-scale automated test systems spread over several years. The executive management team was so pleased with the solution, that they named the room containing the systems after Stan.

The good news is that sales professionals operating in Level 3 revert to Level 2, never to Level 1.

18. Decision-Making Process

To win the business, it is crucial that you understand the decision-making process (DMP) for each of your prospects.

The DMP Group

There are a number of people playing a role in the DMP to select the winning vendor. Let's refer to them as the DMP group, comprised of the approver, the influencers, and the coaches. The sales professional must understand how these DMP members influence one another. The DMP group should not be construed as a formal organization but one that needs to be pieced together by the sales professional much like a jigsaw puzzle. Selling to corporations always involves more than one person in the DMP group. In fact, it's not unusual for it to have more than a dozen DMP members.

Early in the sales cycle, not only does the sales professional lack insights into the DMP's overall makeup, but the group's composition will vary during the sales cycle – two reasons why selling to corporations can be so difficult.

The sales professional can influence a DMP group to add members. Here are two examples how:

- The sales professional arranges for an outside consultant predisposed to his solution to meet with a Senior Executive in the DMP group. If the Senior Executive seeks advice from this consultant, you've effectively placed another person into the DMP group.

- A person in the prospect's organization unaware of the company's plans to make a purchase gets involved after a meeting with the sales professional. This person can become a DMP member.

There are also cases where the sales professional influences the removal of a DMP member. Sales professionals are particularly likely to carry influence if they are the incumbent vendor and have credibility with Senior Executives in the prospect's organization.

Someone from your company, someone from another company acting on your behalf, or one of your consultants needs to have a face-to-face meeting with every DMP member. This is referred to as covering off. DMP members can be found in:

> **Face-to-face meetings with each DMP member is key**

- The prospect's organization
  - User departments
  - HR department
  - Technical evaluation team
  - Executive management team
  - Purchasing department
  - Branch offices

- Consulting companies

- Competitors' companies

- Your company

- Other companies

Because from your very first prospecting call you are attempting to piece together the composition of the DMP group, it is important to capture names dropped during meetings and phone calls. One of these names just might be another key member of the DMP group.

Roles of DMP Members

DMP roles include approver, influencer, and coach. Each DMP member may play one or more of these roles.

Approver

The approver is the final approving authority on purchasing your products, and may be a person, a committee, or a board. In each DMP group, there is only one final approving authority. Anyone

The approver is the final authority on purchasing your products

claiming this status but stating that the decision must be passed upwards, is not the approver (a situation encountered frequently). Identifying the approver is one of the most difficult tasks the sales professional faces.

Most mid- to large-sized companies impose financial approval limits at each management level. One large telecommunications company I encountered with sales exceeding several billion dollars had seven levels of management. Level Four management could approve up to $500,000. If my quote exceeded this amount, I was forced to find the approver at a higher level of management. In small companies, the approver is often the president.

When making sales calls, listen for the approver's name even if you think you know it. If it's not offered, ask for it, from a Senior Executive if possible. But you need to have acquired a degree of credibility before you ask.

Watch for a new approver after a re-organization

Seek this information from low-level management and you run the risk of getting the wrong answers. Few will admit they don't know. Some may point you to the wrong person. A more dangerous and common situation is a low-level manager falsely claiming to be the approver. What a great way to control an unwanted vendor! Prudent sales professionals are continually probing and confirming the approver's name and title. Watch for a change of approver when management re-organizes. As we've emphasized, it's important for you or someone representing your company to have one or more face-to-face meetings with the approver. It almost always shortens the sales cycle.

Influencers

People are called influencers because they influence others in the DMP group. They have the ability to ruin your chances of winning the order, but only the approver can approve it. Influencers can say no to your proposal for any number of reasons, and you often won't know which influencer is the culprit. So work toward persuading each influencer that your solution will satisfy their self-interest. Solving the prospect's corporate pain while satisfying the self-interest of the DMP members is solution selling in action.

> Influencers can only say no; they can't give the final yes

One low-level manager may influence a mid-level manager, who may in turn influence the approver. Another low-level manager may have a direct influence on the approver. Occasionally, you'll find an approver who ignores the advice of would-be influencers.

Coaches

Seasoned sales professionals will tell you that they have always needed coaches to help them understand the DMP. You need to develop at least one coach for each prospect. Coaches are generally found in your prospect's organization, but they can also be found in other companies or with consultants. The sooner you develop your coach, the sooner you'll understand the DMP.

> Develop at least one coach for each prospect

Posture of DMP Members

DMP members assume one of three postures. They are advocates if they want your solution, adversaries if they want a competitor's solution, or non-aligned if they don't care. Your job is to develop advocates, persuade adversaries to be non-aligned or advocates, and convert non-aligned DMP members to be advocates. Your most important task is persuading the approver to be your advocate.

> Persuade the approver to be your advocate

Knowledge Box

You can sum up key information on each DMP member in a Knowledge Box (Figure 14). A quick glance at this box tells you everything you need to know and what you are missing.

DMP Member's Name: Title:	Account Name: Prospect Name:
Role: Approver, Influencer, Coach **Posture:** Advocate, Non-aligned, Adversary	
Corporate Pain: **Self-interest:**	
Influenced By: **Influences Who:**	

Figure 14 DMP Knowledge Box

Influence of DMP Members

Face-to-face calls are the best way to understand the DMP

The influence pattern differs in each DMP group, and can be complex. Understanding how DMP members interact requires much thought and hard work.

The organization chart – a good starting place to determine how DMP members influence one other – is not always easy to obtain, and some companies don't even have one. The sales professional may need to piece together the organization chart much like a jigsaw puzzle. Every time you make a new sales call, you need to understand how that person fits into the puzzle. Suppose your first call is on a Senior Executive. In your questioning, you learn the names of two subordinates you need to meet. You now have three pieces of the puzzle and can initialize the organization chart. Keep adding more names after each sales call. The best way to understand the organization and how the DMP members influence one another is to make many face-to-face calls.

After piecing together the organization chart, you are ready to overlay the lines of influence. The most difficult task in understanding the DMP is determining how each DMP member influences other members. This includes outside influencers such as competitors and consultants. Your coach may be able to help you solve the puzzle. It is not uncommon for a low-level manager to have a direct influence on the approver. Suppose the organization chart shows the chief information officer (CIO) reporting directly to the approver – in this case, the president. It may be that this CIO has little or no influence over the approver, but the organization chart doesn't convey this information. It could be that one of the CIO's direct reports has far more influence on the approver than the CIO.

Other Companies

Often you will discover people in other companies who can influence the DMP group. A like-ranked Senior Executive in another company may know the Senior Executive in your prospect's organization.

Lee, a sales professional, had been unsuccessful in obtaining a meeting with the approver of a mid-sized manufacturing company. Lee's manager knew the president of another manufacturing company located near the targeted company. This president was one of Lee's best-referenced customers. One phone call from Lee's sales manager to the president of the customer led to another phone call from the president of the customer to the president of the prospect, which resulted in Lee getting a meeting with the approver, and closing a sale for $250,000 within one month.

Consultants

Consultants are more active in organizations than ever before, and are often included in the DMP group. You may not even know they are there. How do you find out? Ask. If they are in the DMP group, they are difficult to identify, because their names do not appear on the prospects' organization charts. The only way to determine their presence is to ask. You are vulnerable to losing the order if you don't know what roles consultants are playing.

To determine the presence of consultants, ask

John was a sales professional who had sold a $200,000 product to a farm machinery company. He had an excellent relationship with their chief information officer. Two years later, John was notified of a new requirement in this company and submitted a $500,000 proposal to the CIO, who had been his coach on the previous sale. He lost the business to a competitor who was proposing an inferior product. Years later, John was a district sales manager for another company. At a management meeting, he met a colleague who had been his competitor. When John asked how he had clinched the sale, his colleague replied, "I was working with a consultant in another city who knew the CEO of the farm machinery company. I took him up on his offer to be introduced to the CEO. Within two months, I won the order."

There are several lessons in this story. John relied exclusively on a coach from the previous sale and never considered having someone cover off the approver – in this case, the CEO. The CIO didn't know that a consultant was recommending the competitor's solution to the CEO. Consultants can play a damaging role, as our sales professional found out. John vowed never again to let an approver remain uncovered.

Competition

It is unusual to encounter no competition when angling for a sale. When a company is looking for a new solution, it invariably wants a choice. All sales professionals compete; it's what makes selling challenging and fun.

Important information to know about the competition:

- Names of competitors' companies
- Names of competitors' sales professionals
- Who they are meeting

- Which DMP members favor them and why
- What they are proposing and their price tag

Except for your coach, people don't usually offer this information. You obtain it by listening or by asking questions. Sometimes coaches can shed light on the competition. Assume the competition will be getting the same information about you.

19. Developing the Coach

Sales professionals should develop at least one coach to help them understand each DMP. Otherwise, they'll face a longer sales cycle or lose the order. To be effective, a coach must have credibility with the buying organization, while sales professionals must have credibility with the coach. Where can you find coaches? Usually in the prospect's organization but they may be in other companies including your own. Coaches can be consultants, but beware of tapping friends for the role, unless they have credibility with the buying organization. Start your search for a coach the minute you make your first prospecting call. Among a coach's many tasks is determining what role, if any, consultants play.

> Develop coaches early to shorten the sales cycle

> "Tony, I wouldn't advise calling on Betty now. Call on Bill first, then call on Betty. Make sure you do it in that sequence or you'll likely get yourself in trouble."

A coach can also identify corporate pain or discover the self-interests of some DMP members, and how they influence one another. Sometimes a coach will identify the approver.

Coaches don't like to be compromised; they want to appear impartial, especially if they are in the prospect's organization. Don't advertise your coaching source. Consider meeting him or her off-site, especially if the conversation will deal with personalities and relationships within the DMP.

During the months it takes to develop a coach, you may decide to drop the candidate if you discover he doesn't have credibility with the prospect's organization. Then you'll have to start your search again. It's a mistake to develop a coach who has recently left the prospect's organization, since you don't know whether they left under unfavorable circumstances. If your coach is unable to provide all the information you need, develop a coaching network. Remember, developing a coach early in the sales cycle is one of the sales professional's most important tasks.

A great way to develop your coach is to ask about the roles people play in the DMP. Make your early requests minimal, then gradually escalate them as long as you are receiving positive endorsement from your coach. Each time you take action on a coaching tip, relay the results back to your coach. Feeding results to your coaches increases their interest in seeing you succeed. It's a wonderful human characteristic.

"Thanks, Geraldine. I saw Bill first and did exactly what you said, and I found out what I needed to know. I really appreciate it."

"Well Tony, I've got something more for you now..."

20. Getting to Senior Executives

Watch constantly for introductions to Senior Executives

Sales professionals in the top 20% agree that shortening the sales cycle depends largely on calling high in organizations. One of the most difficult tasks is getting to Senior Executives. Unfortunately, there are no pat rules on how to do this. The best approach is to be constantly watching for opportunities to be introduced to a Senior Executive. The person who can introduce you may be found anywhere: your neighbor, your company's president, a consultant, a Senior Executive from another company. The list goes on and on. You need to have your search radar for Senior Executives turned on all the time.

A successful company had a different sales professional in each office organize a quarterly seminar to find new prospects. These seminars always attracted more than 100 managers from the financial services industry.

Sue, a sales professional in Seattle, used the leverage of these seminars to strike it rich. She obtained her company's approval to contract with a New York consultant well known in the financial services industry, as the keynote speaker at her upcoming seminar. The week following the seminar, Sue decided to take the initiative and call Bill, the CIO of a large financial institution who had attended the seminar. This company already had a large system from Sue's company installed, but the primary vendor was a competitor.

"Hi Bill, what kind of feedback did you get from your people who attended our seminar?"

"It was all very positive, Sue. Everyone from our bank really got a lot out of it. I was very impressed with your keynote speaker's presentation on developing five-year strategic plans."

"Thanks. Bill, I have a suggestion. What if I can convince him to return to Seattle and conduct a similar presentation to your executive management team?"

(Sue had already phoned the New York consultant and obtained his agreement to return to Seattle and deliver a similar presentation if she could win approval from this bank.)

"Let me think about that, Sue."

Six weeks later, the CIO called Sue.

"Sue, I've got something set up for June 5 at 4:00 pm. It will be in our boardroom, and the four Group EVPs will be there. The CEO has asked you to attend, as well."

As the consultant was about to begin his presentation, the CEO interrupted.

"Sue, since you arranged this meeting, I think you should take five or ten minutes to tell us what you are trying to do with our bank."

Sue had anticipated this request, and was well prepared. Both presentations were well received. Two months later, she had another sale from this bank for over $1,000,000, and had forged new relationships with the bank's executive management team.

Why not engage a keynote speaker recognized by your target market for your next seminar? Use this speaker as your springboard to meet Senior Executives.

When you have a successful face-to-face meeting with a Senior Executive early in the sales cycle, he or she will often mention others you should meet and may even indicate the role they will play in evaluating the proposal.

"Betty, what is Rod's role in the evaluation of the proposal?"

"Rod plays a key role as the chairman of the evaluation committee."

"What major issues should I be discussing with him?"

Sue gets to meet another Senior Executive.

Sue was following up on an inquiry from a small privately held telecom company. During her first meeting, she asked a mid-level manager for a copy of its most recent annual report. The manager excused himself to obtain a copy. Five minutes later, he returned and said the president would not approve giving her the annual report.

Several weeks after this call, Sue's CEO invited her to a large conference of presidents of high-tech companies. She noted that the president of the small telecom company was on the list of attendees. She described her previous prospecting call on the mid-level manager to her CEO.

Her firm drew up a strategy for Sue to be introduced by her CEO to the president of this telecom company at the conference. As soon as she was introduced, the telecom CEO said:

"Oh, you're the salesperson who called on us last week and I refused to let my people give you our annual report."

After a short conversation, he said:

"Sue, there will be an annual report in the mail tomorrow. Drop in to see me next week."

Two months later, she sold the company two computer systems valued at $500,000. She was lucky that her sales-oriented CEO invited her to this conference. Many others wouldn't have bothered.

Always look for opportunities to meet CEOs, presidents and Senior Executives, or have someone at that level in your organization do so.

21. Brainstorming

Brainstorming is an exercise to develop creative solutions for many of your sales problems. Ideas can come so fast that you may need two people to write them down.

District sales meetings can be a great forum for brainstorming. A sales professional looking for an action plan to close a sale decides to lead a brainstorming session, and discovers many valuable ideas during the process. At later district sales meetings, other sales professionals lead brainstorming sessions to arrive at their solutions. This is a great team-building exercise, as sales professionals in the district help one another.

Include employees from sales support, customer service, marketing, etc., to add another dimension to the session. It may be the administrative assistant or someone in the order processing department who contributes a winning idea. In smaller companies, the president often participates. The rule of thumb is that anyone who touches the prospect in any way is a candidate to participate in the brainstorming session.

How to Brainstorm

- Define the sales problem

- Let the ideas flow

- Don't be judgmental

- Use short, succinct statements

- Think fast; don't reflect

- Capture ideas on flip charts

- Attach completed flip charts to walls with masking tape

- Encourage outrageous ideas

- The best ideas come out of the outrageous ideas of others

- Participants raise their hands as soon as they have an idea

- Don't hold back any of your own ideas

- Go with the flow; one idea will lead to another

- Don't stay with one train of thought for too long

- Go for quantity, not quality, as you'll miss some of the best ideas

- Brainstorming can take an hour or more

- Stop the brainstorming when ideas slow to a trickle

- Don't discuss the brainstorm items until all have been posted

At the end of the brainstorming session, you may have twenty to 100 items. Now the challenge is to separate the wheat from the chaff. Triage each item by assigning A to essential items, B to important information not requiring action, and C to the remaining items (chaff).

22. The Sales Plan

By the time your prospect arrives near the middle of the FUNNEL, you should have evolved a sales plan that includes the sales strategy. A strategy may be as simple as having a sales objective, or could take up to a dozen pages and include an action plan to close the sale on a major account valued at millions of dollars. The strategy should be updated continuously as you and fellow sales team members interact with DMP members.

The Sales Objective

Have a realistic sales objective for each prospect early in the sales cycle – one that is well thought-out, realistic, and succinct, maximum two short sentences. If you have a large number of prospects, how can you possibly remember all the sales objectives without recording them? By writing them down, you help your sales team know what you are trying to accomplish. The sales objective must include:

Have a realistic sales objective for each prospect

- Prospect's name

- Dollar value of the sale

- Date order is expected

Example:

> "Obtain an order from ABC Company for $150,000 by August 31, 200X. There will be an upgrade of $250,000 within eighteen months of the initial order."

Action Plan to Close the Sale

If one of your prospects gets stuck in the lower half of your FUNNEL, consider creating a more detailed plan to close the order. This is called the action plan and works best as a spreadsheet. The action plan lists all the actions needed to close the sale, in short sentences containing an action verb.

They should be:

Specific

Measurable

Action-oriented

Realistic

Time related

Obtain an order from ABC Company for $150,000 by August 31, 200X. There will be an upgrade of $250,000 within eighteen months of initial order.

Item #	Action Item	Person(s) Responsible	Planned Date	Actual Date
1	Meet approver to verify budget	DT	March 10	March 11
2	Discuss benefits with CIO	DT	March 15	
3	Other	DT/BD	March 18	
4	Other	JK	March 31	
5	Other	DT	April 9	

Figure 15 Action Plan to Close the Sale

The action items are listed chronologically, indicating the persons responsible, the planned date of execution, and the actual date of completion (Figure 15). It's a good idea to reinforce the purpose of the action plan by placing the sales objective above the action plan.

Number the action items if you are sharing your action plan with your sales team, or if you are part of a global major-account sales team. It's easier to refer to items #21 and #25 than to waste time while the other person is searching for them by name.

The best way to create this action plan is to lead a short brainstorming session with your sales team and others with a vested interest in winning this business. Include your sales manager if you feel that will add value.

Plan the order of your sales calls

It's important to execute the actions in a certain order. If you learn that the next person you need to meet has just gone on a three-week vacation – potentially stalling your selling cycle by three weeks, you can get yourself in an awkward situation by calling on the wrong person at the wrong time. The order in which DMP members receive information can be critical.

Cost of Ownership Analysis

Experienced sales professionals never criticize the competition, even by inference. The cost of ownership analysis allows you to avoid doing this by helping your prospect compare the proposals objectively on an apples-to-apples basis.

> Use the cost of ownership analysis to win the business

This analysis involves designing a spreadsheet detailing product costs and all the other initial and lifetime costs. First, set up columns for the "Cost Item Name," "Your Company's Proposal," and each "Competitor's Proposal." If your prospect has named competitors, insert the names at the top of the appropriate column; otherwise, use a format similar to Figure 16. Next, place the name of each cost item in the first column. You may end up with more than a dozen cost item names. Third, insert your costs for each item in the second column. Finally, present the cost of ownership analysis to your prospect. Ask them to obtain the competitor's costs and insert them in the appropriate column. You defeat the entire purpose of the cost of ownership analysis if you insert or supply the competitors' costs yourself. Your prospects will have ownership of this analysis only if they obtain the itemized costs from your competition. The second-to-last row of the spreadsheet represents each proposal's cost of ownership. The last row may show the ROI of each.

Cost Item Name	Your Company's Proposal	Competitor A Proposal	Competitor B Proposal
Product Costs	$250,000	$290,000	$220,000
Mainteneance Costs (3 yrs.)	$75,000	$105,000	$180,000
Other Costs	$200,000	$250,000	$250,000
Cost of Ownership	$525,000	$645,000	$650,000
ROI	14%	11.5%	11.7%

Figure 16 Cost of Ownership Analysis

Notice that Competitor B, with the lowest product costs, probably won't win the business because it has the highest cost of ownership.

Costs associated with the life cycle of the product (such as maintenance costs) often significantly reduce your proposal's cost of ownership. The cost of ownership analysis allows your prospect to discover the true cost of purchasing each vendor's product without your having to discuss the competition. It is crucial for you to know what your competitors are proposing. And your prospect will realize that you would offer this cost of ownership analysis only if you had earned the right and were confident you had the winning proposal.

Asking for the Order

> Asking for the order can uncover hidden objections

The importance of asking for the order may be obvious to salespersons, but it is surprising how many don't, or who ask prematurely. It's all about earning the right. You have earned the right if you are certain that the DMP members are very clear that your proposal satisfies their needs. If you are not sure, you have more homework to do. Ask for the order because it not only gives you an opportunity to close, but it uncovers any hidden objections.

"Betty, based on our discussions over the past six months, would you like to proceed?"

"Tony, I'm really concerned about one of my direct reports. He just doesn't feel comfortable that your solution will help him achieve his numbers."

"If I can convince Bob that our proposal will help him achieve his numbers, would you be prepared to place an order?"

"Tony, if you can do that, you've got a deal."

Sometimes it takes more than a year to earn the right to ask the most important question when selling to corporations.

23. Selling to Committees

Selling to corporations often involves selling to committees. The larger the company, the greater the likelihood of finding committees. They can be selection committees, evaluation committees, technical review committees, etc., and all can play a part in the DMP. You may think the vote of the committee is the vote of the majority, but it's not necessarily the case. These committees are headed by a chairperson who may or may not be a power broker. Power brokers are defined as persons with the greatest influence on the other committee members. Not only can there be more than one power broker within a committee, but these power brokers may be influenced by an outside consultant. Identifying power brokers on a committee is another major challenge facing the sales professional.

> **Identify the committee's power brokers**

Lee, a sales professional, had been invited to make a product presentation on a system to the selection committee of a Midwestern university. There was a sense of urgency, as the system had to be ordered, installed, and readied for student use in ten weeks. The committee was predisposed to the competitor, as a number of their systems were installed around the campus. After the morning presentations, the two competing sales professionals waited in the library while the committee made the selection. First the chairman called the competition into his office to announce the winning vendor. Then he informed Lee that the decision had been made overwhelmingly in favor of the competitor, and the purchase requisition was in purchasing already. The committee chairman, highly regarded and influential on campus, apologized profusely, stating that he really wanted this contract to be awarded to Lee's company – that he preferred Lee's product and knew his president. After two more apologies from the chairman, Lee finally picked up on the opportunity and asked, "What could we have done to win this business?" The chairman replied, "If your proposal had been under $100,000, I could have convinced the committee to recommend your system." Lee then asked, "If I could do this for you right now, would you call purchasing and tell them to cancel the purchase requisition?" The surprised chairman agreed. The sales professional called his company from the phone on the chairman's desk and obtained permission to ship the system for $99,000 and deliver it in eight weeks. The chairman immediately cancelled the requisition and told Lee he could pick up the purchase order the next morning. The system was installed eight weeks later. In this case, the chairman was the power broker and chose to overrule the committee's unanimous decision. An order is not an order until the product is installed and paid for.

It is still prudent to influence the voting majority, as this is how most committees reach decisions.

24. The Sales Call

The sales call is still the best method for obtaining information to develop your sales strategies. Sales calls are defined as face-to-face calls with your prospects.

Sales Call Objectives

These are the specific objectives you wish to accomplish on each sales call. The more specific objectives you can accomplish on each call, the shorter the sales cycle.

> **Every sales call must have one or more objectives**

Every sales call must have at least one sales call objective, usually derived from the sales criteria and the action plan. To ensure they are well thought out, write them down before the sales call. Another benefit: individuals making the call with you will be very clear on what you want to accomplish and which objectives, if any, will be their respective responsibility.

By making your sales call objectives specific and measurable, you obtain more detailed information to update the sales strategy. If the objectives are vague and open-ended, it may take you a year instead of six months to close a sale. Sales professionals who average six sales call objectives on each sales call will close business faster than those who average only one or two.

Examples of call objectives:

- Determine latest date that the new application must be operational.
- Determine details of any consultants playing a role in the DMP.
- Obtain agreement to initialize a joint implementation plan.

If you are an early morning person, make your most difficult sales calls in the morning when you perform the best, and ask for a morning meeting to help you maximize results.

Remember: establish specific sales call objectives for each sales call to significantly shorten the sales cycle.

Using Agendas Effectively

Amazingly, many salespeople don't bother to use a written agenda for their sales calls. Once you develop the habit of using agendas for all your sales calls, you'll be able to prepare them in a few minutes reaping many benefits accordingly:

Use a written agenda for all sales calls

- facilitates two-way communication
- assists in preparing for the call
- assists you in leading the call
- maximizes the results of the meeting
- enhances joint call transitions
- differentiates you from the competition
- allows DMP members to review the call

If you send the agenda in advance, be cautious with faxes. Your competitor's advocate may be standing beside the fax machine. An e-mail attachment is far safer.

Take one or two extra copies of the agenda in case others are invited at the last moment.

Sales Call Agenda

Differentiate yourself from competitive salespeople by using sales call agendas on all your sales calls, using your company's first page letterhead. How often do business cards get filed away never to be seen again? Let your sales call agenda become another source for your prospects to contact you. If your prospects file copies into a folder on your company, this might make it easier for them to obtain this contact information.

Mardon Marketing Company Inc.

ABC Company Inc.
Betty Green
President

June 28, 200X

- Discuss ABC's strategic relationships
- Arrange head office visit
- Financial measurement
- Review management presentation results
- Overview of Mardon Marketing solutions
- Next steps
-

31X Cordova Drive • Seattle, WA 9800X • Phone: (206) 656-001X • Fax: (206) 656-002X
openshow@keepingthefunnelfull.com   www.keepingthefunnelfull.com

Figure 17 Sample Agenda – Sales Call

The heading is centered at the top of the agenda (Figure 17) and includes:

- Name of prospect's company
- Names and titles of people attending from prospect
- Date of call

It is a good idea to use titles, because some people are sensitive if titles are omitted, but there is no need to include the names of persons representing your company on the agenda. Use a smaller font for the date. Describe each agenda item up to about seven words, in bullet format, double spaced for aesthetics, readability, and note-taking. List items pertaining to the prospect first, because they are the most important and you want to be viewed as the sales professional more interested in the prospect's issues than in just selling your products. Finally, add one blank bullet as the last agenda item.

Introducing the Agenda

Introducing the agenda is the best way to transition into the business part of the meeting. Take 15 to 20 seconds to outline agenda items; this gives those attending a heads-up on the direction the meeting will flow. Don't read the agenda items; paraphrase them. If you haven't done this before, it's worth practicing. After paraphrasing, obtain their agreement to proceed with the meeting. When you have introduced the last agenda item, the blank bullet comes into play.

> Use a blank bullet as the last agenda item

After introducing the agenda, the dialogue might be:

"Does that sound okay to you Betty?"

"Sure does; let's do it."

"I've placed a blank bullet here, in case you might like to add another item."

Roughly 25% of the time they will add another item, often the most important discussion item on their mind – one of which you've been unaware, and took a while to occur to them. They may need more than three seconds to respond, so give them ten seconds, and you might hit the jackpot. Paraphrase the new item in a few words, and ask if you have understood correctly. Ask if you might insert it into their copy beside the blank bullet at the bottom of the agenda, then add it to your copy. All this will take about fifteen seconds. This last bullet is where you will start the meeting.

Using the Agenda

> **Go to the next item only when the prospect is ready**

If you haven't been given a new topic, start your meeting with the first agenda item. When it's finished, move to the next. But don't go blindly onto the next item without getting some kind of tacit approval by eye contact, a nod of the head, or a statement such as:

> "Is it okay to go on?"

If a new item was added, stay with it as long as the person is willing to discuss it. When it is finished, go to your first item at the top of the agenda.

If you move too quickly to the next item without approval, you might be giving up an opportunity to learn some critical information. If someone drops a name or says something important, write it on your copy of the agenda while they are talking. Stay focused on their issues as long as they wish to talk about them. Don't rush them. Use open-ended questions so you can delve deeper into issues. The first agenda item may end up being the most important part of the meeting. On the other hand, you can spend the entire meeting on one agenda item and never get to others. If this happens, ask if they would rather continue or schedule another meeting. If the meeting has gone well, you're more than likely to get approval on continuing or rescheduling.

List of Questions

Why is it so important to have a list of questions for your sales calls? Few people can remember the dozen or more questions they need to ask, or the best order in which to ask them. How many times have you returned to your office after the sales call and realized that you forgot to ask two key questions? Your list of questions pre-empts this.

During the sales call, focus your attention on the prospect – something you can't do if you are writing copious notes on the prospect's answers. If you're writing, you're not listening, not offering adequate eye contact, not returning acknowledgement or nods to show that you are interested in what the person is saying. In short, you just won't be engaged.

To ensure proper engagement, leave a one-inch blank space between each question to allow you to insert short, encoded notes such as key words, names dropped, hieroglyphics, doodles, diagrams, or anything else that will remind you of answers to your questions. Towards the end of the sales call, glance at your list of questions to check that there are no blank spaces. Now you know you are leaving the meeting with all the answers.

Leave a one-inch space below each question

Convert these encoded notes into full explanations within minutes of the sales call if possible; otherwise, you will forget the connection or meaning. In other words, complete the call report as soon as possible. Memory for necessary details typically fades fast; an hour's lapse can erase valuable information.

Convert the encoded notes within minutes after the call

Some questions will apply to the agenda items and should appear in the same order. Questions independent of the agenda items may be interspersed. Ensure that you have harmonized the agenda and list of questions as much as possible. And listen carefully; sometimes the prospect will answer several questions at the same time.

Sue, our sales professional, had made two previous sales calls on the approver of a small company. Because he was to be traveling extensively, she obtained his agreement to e-mail a list of questions she had prepared for their next meeting. One week later, Sue received a three-page e-mail answering all the questions in much more detail than she would have obtained on the sales call.

Place your list of questions on the inside front cover of your hard-copy notebook before making the call. At the beginning of the meeting, your list of questions will guide you in a professional manner through your sales call.

Resist the temptation to give the list of questions to the prospect. It is more effective to obtain the answers interactively. Like everything else in sales, there are exceptions to this guideline.

Open and Close-Ended Questions

During your sales calls, constantly seek more information about the corporate pain, the DMP, and the self-interests of the DMP members – preferably using a combination of well thought-out open and close-ended questions. Open-ended questions allow the person to elaborate, while close-ended questions elicit only one- or two-word answers.

Open-ended questions

"What challenges must be overcome to increase your productivity?"

"What strategies have you developed to meet those challenges?"

"What criteria do you use to evaluate your vendors?"

"What are the major factors leading to your company's success?"

Close-ended questions

"Would it be appropriate for me to meet with Betty?"

"Would you mention that I will be contacting her?"

"Would you introduce me to her?"

"What is the size of your sales force?"

Open-ended questions often result in the person dropping names of unknown DMP members. These are people you need to meet. If the same name is mentioned several times, it is even more important to meet with them. Use the onion-peeling technique to obtain more information about these new names.

"What is Jane Peters' role in your organization?" (open-ended)

"Would she be involved in the selection process?" (close-ended)

"Do you think it would be useful for me to meet Jane?" (close-ended)

"Would you mention that I'll be contacting her?" (close-ended)

"Would you introduce me to her?" (close-ended)

Remember to write on your agenda or your list of questions the names of all people mentioned (names dropped). If you are making a joint call, remind the others to record any names they hear, in case you miss them. The quality of your questioning and your ability to listen will help move the sales process forward.

Active Listening

Active listening involves paraphrasing statements to confirm your understanding of what was just said. Do this accurately, and the person will immediately know you have grasped the exact meaning and are a careful listener. If you don't get it right, the client can correct your interpretation to clarify your understanding. Active listening is not always easy; it requires practice. Overused, active listening can be annoying.

Rules for Asking a Question

Lee, a new sales professional, was near the end of his six-month sales training program. As a student, he was required to make a practice sales call on executives of his company. These one-hour sales calls were videotaped and critiqued by the sales trainers, in front of the executives and class. During Lee's critique, he was admonished by a legendary sales trainer for asking an embarrassing question of the executive on whom he was calling. At the end of the training program, the trainer took Lee aside, and after a short apology for making an example of him, he gave Lee a wallet-sized card containing the Rules for Asking a Question. The trainer suggested that Lee read them over and over again, to register them into his subconscious and to make it easier to apply the rules. For the next several months, Lee read these questions for two or three minutes just before arriving for his sales call. The longer the elevator ride in the office building, the more time he had to review these questions. He still reviews them today, and is one of the top sales producers for a large company.

1. Think about the question
   - Does it make sense?
   - Do you need to know the answer?
   - Do they know the answer?
   - Will you embarrass them?
   - Will the answer make them look good?

2. Don't make a speech

3. Don't answer the question in the process of asking it

4. Ask one question at a time

5. Don't interrupt them when they are answering it

Figure 18 Rules for Asking a Question

The meaning of the rules for asking a question is self-evident (Figure 18). Of all the rules, the one most often violated is, "Ask one question at a time." When you observe a person asking a string of two to six questions in a row, with no breaks, guess which questions get answered? Yes, it's almost always the last question and occasionally, it might be the last two.

> **Ask one question at a time**

A sales manager was interviewing a salesperson for a sales position. During the interview, he noticed that the candidate would ask a string of questions without waiting for the answers. One time, the sales manager counted six questions and observed that he was answering only the last one. He pointed out to the candidate that he had just asked six questions in a row, and challenged him to tell him how many answers he'd received. The candidate replied that he wasn't sure. Imagine this same salesperson making a sales call and missing the answers to the first five questions! Clearly any one of the unanswered questions might have uncovered the corporate pain. Naturally, the sales manager removed this candidate from the short list.

Next time you are watching a television interview, pay attention to the questioning techniques, and watch how often only the last question gets answered.

Closing on Objections

Objections from the DMP members are necessary to winning the sale during the sales process. If you're getting agreement on everything, this is not a good sign. The axiom No Objections = No Sale is as true today as it ever was.

> **No Objections = No Sale**

During sales calls, the sales professional should listen carefully for objections, which indicate some interest in your solution. In the phrase "closing on objections," the close doesn't always mean asking for the order. Many incremental closes must occur on the way to closing an order.

If a DMP member states:

"I've heard from your competition that your company is not committed to staying in this business."

You have just been presented with a valid objection. Closing on this objection might be:

"If my president informed you personally that he is committed to staying in this business for the long term, would you still consider us in your selection process?"

Joint Sales Calls

Sometimes it is necessary to take other people on joint sales calls. Your prospect should know in advance who else will be coming and the reasons why they are there. If you have already booked an appointment and discover later that you would like to include others, be sure to contact the prospect to explain the change. Mention the names of others you would like to bring and why they are coming. Most people don't like to be surprised when you show up with other persons, and they were expecting only you.

Each person on the joint call must know the objectives of the sales call. They should be given a copy of the agenda indicating any items assigned to them. For the call to run smoothly, your people should understand how and when the transitions will take place. For important calls, consider a practice role play with someone in your office posing as the prospect, using the agenda and the list of questions.

On other occasions, it is neither convenient nor appropriate for the sales professional to be present on a sales call. For example, don't attend if you feel that there would be a better exchange of information between two Senior Executives of like-rank. It is your responsibility as account manager to brief your Senior Executive on the sales objective and the sales call objectives.

The person leading the call determines who has responsibility for each agenda item and how the transitions will take place. A worst-case scenario is when two persons making the joint call both think they are leading the call. This usually results in a disaster.

Account Manager

The sales professional responsible for the prospect – the account manager – establishes the reasons for all sales calls and who should attend. This is the concept of account control, which is lost when others in the selling company contact DMP members without first discussing it with the account manager. The person leading the call (not necessarily the account manager), manages the agenda but it is the account manager who decides who will lead all the sales calls. If you are taking a Senior Executive to meet a Senior Executive in the prospect's organization, keep in mind that the call may be more effective if led by your Senior Executive. In this case, your only role would be to make the introductions, then turn the agenda over to your Senior Executive.

> The account manager establishes the objectives for all sales calls

The account manager might say:

> "Mike, this is how I've planned the call. Since most of the agenda items are yours, I'd appreciate it if you would lead this call."

25. The Call Report

Execution

Every sales professional understands the need to make many face-to-face sales calls to obtain important information on the road to winning the sale. What many don't realize is how quickly they forget this important information. It may be forgotten in seconds, minutes, or hours. Writing the call report at the end of the day is not nearly as effective as writing it immediately after the call. Making notes during the call helps, but you cannot

> Write the call report within minutes after the call

record every spoken word. This is why writing a call report within minutes of the sales call can significantly increase what you remember. Ideally, you should be writing it as you are going down the elevator but obviously this is not practical.

As you enter a building to make a sales call, pick out a quiet location in the lobby or nearby coffee shop to write the call report, immediately after the meeting. Reserve five or ten minutes to do so.

You'll save time if you already have a call report template. Once the call report has captured key information, you can focus exclusively on your next sales call.

Information for your call report comes from the following sources.

- cryptic notes and names dropped on your list of questions

- cryptic notes and names dropped on your agenda

- comments from others on a joint call

Contact management or spreadsheet software helps in setting up call reports. Consider creating an electronic call reports folder for each prospect. Call reports are for your eyes only, and should be shared only with others in your company who need to know. They are not meant for outsiders, as they almost always contain sensitive information.

Benefits

Call reports will trigger new ideas and actions

Information obtained during your sales calls can be of inestimable value on the journey to winning the order. What if you completed call reports for six sales calls made on two or three different people from the same company over a period of four months? You certainly wouldn't remember everything that happened without your reports. If you review all of them in the fifth month, however, you might find they shed light on:

- a new or updated sales strategy

- people you need to meet

- where the next sales call should be

- another potential coach

- important information for your presentations or proposal

You'll likely get more out of reviewing call reports in hard copy than on the screen, since to improve your understanding, you will probably need to go back and forth between related reports just as you do when reading related articles in a newspaper.

When you've obtained agreement to make a presentation, review all your call reports, because they will remind you of ideas to include. A call report's usefulness becomes particularly evident for team selling in multiple locations or countries. Imagine the synergy when a major account sales team posts all call reports to a password-protected website. In such a scenario, sales management and the major account team are always current on the status of each prospect.

Many sales managers appreciate being kept informed through call reports from their sales professionals. It's simply the best instrument for initiating dialogue, and helps you take the sales strategy to the next level.

It gets even better. As you read those six call reports, sometimes you'll get lucky and find that they spur you to ask permission to submit an unsolicited proposal. If your prospect agrees, you have an excellent chance to win the business without competitors knowing until it is too late. You've also pre-empted the client going out to a Request for Proposal (RFP).

How can salespeople say they can't spare five to ten minutes to complete a call report when it may be worth its weight in gold?

Composition

The call report template is easy to design and hastens the recording process (Figure 19). The entire sales force should use the same format.

Call Report

Date:

Prospect Name:

Names and Titles:

1.

2.

3.

Call Objectives:

1.

2.

3.

Call Results:

1.

2.

3.

Action Items:

By Client:

1.

2.

By You:

1.

2.

Names Dropped:

1.

2.

Next Meeting:

Challenges/Objections/Comments:

Figure 19 Call Report Template

Before the Sales Call

Complete the top half of the call report before you make the call.

Date

This is the date of the call.

Prospect Name

This is the name of the company you will be meeting. If you have more than one prospect inside the company, you may wish to identify each prospect with a specific name, i.e. ABC Company – Prospect 1.

Names and Titles

Include the name and title of everyone attending from the prospect's organization, as well as the name, title, and company name of any third-party attendees, plus the names of everyone representing your company. List the prospect's personnel first, and in order of position.

Call Objectives

The call objectives are what you want to accomplish during the sales call – typically, one to six for each sales call. Building rapport doesn't count as a call objective, because it's not specific; it's something you should be doing on every call. A day or so before the call, take time to think through the call objectives and list them on the template.

More call objectives:

- Determine the names of the evaluation team.

- Describe the process used by the evaluation team to make the decision to buy.

- Obtain Ms. Green's agreement to visit our head office.

- Obtain agreement to make a presentation to the executive management team.

After the Sales Call
Call Results

There should be a one-to-one correspondence between the call objectives and call results. Call objective No. 3 produces call result No. 3.

Action Items

Successful sales professionals ensure that both parties agree to take specific actions in the days or weeks following the sales call. You need to capture these action items on the call report. Be sure to include a summary of these action items as a reminder in your thank you letter.

Names Dropped

During the dialogue, listen for names dropped. It's easy to miss one when you are focused on listening and on thinking what you should say next. Capture such names on the call report, including, if possible, their role in the DMP. This new DMP member could lead you closer to the sale.

Challenges/Objections/Comments

Other important information discovered during the sales call.

26. The Proposal

At some point during the selling process, you need to submit a proposal. Compared with the competition, your proposal should provide the most cost-effective solution to solve the corporate pain. Consider placing "confidential" at the top of each page. If you have included any intellectual property, you copyright your proposal.

Communicating the Financial Justification

The financial section of your proposal helps the approver justify selecting your solution. The return on investment (ROI) is a common method used to financially evaluate proposals.

$$ROI (\%) = \frac{(Total\ cash\ flows - Investment)}{Investment} \times 100$$

It's up to you to know how your prospect establishes financial justification for its purchases, and to base your financial justification on your prospect's methods. Obtain this information from the approver or, failing that, from one of his or her direct reports.

If you and your competitors' proposals result in higher ROIs than those in the proposals for an unrelated project, the prospect may elect to fund only this unrelated project.

The Executive Summary

The executive summary is the most important component of your proposal. This is the place to include key points differentiating your solution from the competitor's. Written for the approver, it should highlight the principal reasons why the prospect should acquire your product. Approvers, be they the president or a Senior Executive, are extremely busy people, and may not have time to read much of your proposal. In fact, some of them don't get past the first page. Make it easy for them by placing the Executive Summary on the first page.

> The executive summary is the most important component of the proposal

If you have only two or three significant reasons why the prospect should choose your product, present them in short paragraphs. Present a larger number of reasons as bullets. In either case, make the first item the financial justification for selecting your solution, because this is always the most important issue for the approver. Be sure to express it by the same financial evaluation method the prospect uses.

Executive Summary Guidelines

- Target it for the approver

- Use one or two pages

- Draft it after proposal is written

- Place it on first page of proposal

- Make financial justification of your solution the first item

- List other reasons in order of importance

- State how your proposal satisfies the corporate pain

- Indicate how all mandatory requirements (RFP) are satisfied

- Exclude minor reasons

- Include only information embedded in the proposal

- Include a benefit for each member of the evaluation team

Request for Proposal

RFPs arriving out of the blue rarely result in orders

How should the sales professional handle a RFP received before she has developed a business relationship in the buying organization? Large companies and governments issue RFPs, and unexpected ones can cause a lot of grief, while few result in an order. It can take weeks or months to answer RFPs; most are wired for competitors who have developed relationships within the buying organization already. Be involved with the prospect early to specify at least one unique feature of your product as a mandatory requirement. It makes the time spent responding worthwhile, as you'll stand a better chance of winning the business than you will responding to RFPs that arrive out of the blue.

Lee's sales manager presented him with a 200-page RFP from a large company. Lee told his manger that he couldn't answer it unless the firm arranged for him to meet with one of the prospect's Senior Executives (someone known to the sales manager). Lee, a sales veteran, knew intuitively that the probability of winning this business was almost zero, because he didn't know the people or their issues. His manager arranged the meeting, which involved flying more than a thousand miles. After spending three days with his prospect's staff, Lee developed a rapport with the evaluation team and learned what issues were important to them. On returning to his office, he spent several weeks writing the proposal and won an order for over a million dollars. Lee believes he won this business because he insisted on meeting key personnel at the pilot site before writing the RFP response. Otherwise, it would have been a futile academic exercise. Luckily, Lee had a supportive manager.

Unsolicited Proposal

When you've satisfied the following conditions, you have earned the right to request permission to submit an unsolicited proposal:

- You have full knowledge of the corporate pain

- Key DMP members know you understand the corporate pain

- You have identified the self-interest of each key DMP member

- The prospect knows it is not in their best interest to issue an RFP

If you obtain this permission, it can give you an inside track to winning the order. Submit this request to the approver or a key DMP member. You would like the proposal to be unsolicited, because this will shorten the sales cycle and likely eliminate the competition; the competitors usually won't know what's happened until it is too late. If your prospect is required to go the RFP route, you're still well positioned to win the order. One last point: almost everyone wants a choice when making a decision. Do your prospect the favor by giving them two variants of your unsolicited proposal.

Initiating a Joint Implementation Plan

Most salespeople think that an implementation plan covers only the post sales activities, and the new customer initiates it shortly after the purchase order is issued. Why not take the initiative near the middle

Initiate a joint implementation plan near the middle of the sales cycle

of the sales cycle and suggest to your prospect that you develop a joint implementation together?

> "Betty, I've taken the liberty of starting an implementation plan to ensure that your company will have a successful experience with our solution. May I briefly review it with you to determine what activities are missing?"
>
> "Tony, I think that's great idea. Why don't you leave it with me and we'll review it together at our next meeting?"

From that moment on, Tony ensures that an agenda item each meeting covers what Betty calls "updating the implementation plan." One of the activities included in the implementation plan is "order issued." Betty has now seen how Tony will help her team ensure a successful implementation. Tony is well positioned to win this business because his competitors probably have not thought of taking the same initiative. He may even decide to include the joint implementation plan as an appendix to his proposal.

27. The Real Reasons for Losing a Sale

There are a number of real reasons for losing a sale, but most sales professionals agree that the following are the major culprits.

Not Verifying a Budget

In one of the worst case scenarios, salespeople find themselves spending six months to a year attempting to close a prospect with no success. They've made dozens of sales calls and written a detailed proposal, only to find that there were no funds budgeted in the first place.

Astute sales professionals listen for signals that verify a budget from their very first prospecting call. Early in the sales cycle and before the proposal is written, they confirm with Senior Executives that a budget exists and its upper limit. The best person to verify budget information is the approver. Failing this, confirm the budget number with another Senior Executive. Don't write a proposal or answer an RFP until you confirm a budget is available. It is so important to develop relationships with Senior Executives controlling the budgets, as they are the only ones who have the right answers. Too many salespeople ask a middle manager if there is a budget and later find they lost the order because they were misinformed. They asked the wrong person.

> **Don't write the proposal until you've verified the budget**

It's a recipe for failure to write a detailed proposal before verifying the budget. If no budget exists, extricate yourself early, when the prospect is near the top of the FUNNEL.

> **No budget, no sale**

"Betty, can you verify if funding has been approved for this project?"

"Yes it has, Tony, but we are going to budget it over the next two fiscal years."

"What amount has been budgeted for each year?"

"We've put $275,000 towards it next year and at least $375,000 for the second year."

"Thanks for sharing that information with me Betty. Who will be the final approving authority?"

"I will."

Your sales management may ask you:

"Tell me in detail how you determined their budget."

"Who did you ask?"

"What is their position in the organization?"

"What exactly did they say?"

"Who else has confirmed this budget?"

"Who is the approver?"

You need to have the answers to these questions even if your management doesn't ask them. If there is no budget, there is no sale.

It's not unusual for RFPs to omit budget information which may be known to the purchasing department. Don't forget to maintain a friendly business relationship with purchasing.

Approver Not Covered

> **Ensure someone representing your company meets with the approver**

Your chances of winning the order are much higher if someone representing your company has met with the approver sometime during the sales cycle. You may be sure that your competitor has taken this action.

Level Locked

Suppose you are working at a trade show and meet a low-level manager at your booth. You're elated because you think you have found a new prospect. After several meetings, you know it is time to meet with the appropriate Senior Executive. When you ask to be introduced, one of the following scenarios will likely occur:

- The manager says there is no reason for you to meet with the Senior Executive and you should deal only with him (level locked).

- The manager states that he will keep the Senior Executive up to date on your proposed solution (level locked).

- The manager has little or no credibility inside his organization and couldn't get you introduced even if he tried (may be level locked).

- The manager agrees to make the introduction (not level locked).

Don, a sales professional with a small computer company, was working the booth at a trade show when he met Charlotte, a level-one manager with a large telecommunications company. After a follow-up meeting, he had a new prospect sitting in Phase 1 of his FUNNEL.

Charlotte was responsible for writing specifications for an RFP to be issued in four months. Don had proved to Charlotte that one of the mandatory specifications was unnecessary. She agreed to change it, which allowed him to bid on this million-dollar contract. About the same time, she told him to deal exclusively with her on all matters pertaining to this RFP. He was now level locked.

Writing the proposal consumed two months' effort by the sales team, which won a spot on the short list. About this time, Charlotte suggested that if Don's company was awarded the order, it might be nice to have the two teams celebrate with an evening cruise party.

Winning the order depended on winning the benchmark – an expensive proposition for this small company, as it would have to purchase thirty large disk drives from a supplier in order to run the benchmark. On one of his trips to head office, the president asked, "Don, what are you doing trying to close a million-dollar order by dealing exclusively with the lowest level of management?" After convincing the president that he could win the order despite being level locked, his company ordered the disks. Several weeks after winning the benchmark, his company was awarded a million-dollar order. During the celebration cruise, the approver presented a package to Don, a large pizza box containing a chocolate chip cookie with the purchase order number spelled out in M&M candies. Whoever said that purchase orders have to be written on paper?

There is an exception to every axiom in selling. If Don had gone upstairs, Charlotte would likely have made it difficult for him to win the business. She certainly wouldn't have changed the mandatory specification. Fortunately, Don had sufficient prospects in his FUNNEL that he would have achieved quota without this million-dollar order.

Another worst-case scenario is when the low-level manager says:

"Don't worry about calling on Betty; I'll deal with her."

This low-level manager thinks he can do your selling for you, which negates any influence you could have on others in the DMP group. Once a low-level manager assumes your selling responsibilities, you no longer have control of the sale. You'll feel handcuffed. What makes selling so difficult is that exceptions exist for every rule as the Charlotte story illustrates.

Consider another scenario. After a number of meetings with a low-level manager, you have concluded that the only way to determine the corporate pain is from the Senior Executive. Your fear is that you will get a negative answer if you ask the low-level manager to introduce you upstairs. If you then try to meet with the Senior Executive, you run the risk of upsetting the low-level manager. Managers have an uncanny way of learning about these end-runs. They may go out of their way to ensure that you don't get the meeting, or may be mad enough to prevent you winning the sale. You are in a very difficult situation.

Like-ranked selling avoids getting level locked

One way to avoid getting level locked is engaging in like-ranked selling. This method uses your management for meetings with like-ranked management in the buying organization. Once the sales professional has determined the organizational level of the approver, he requests a like-ranked manager from his own company to make the call.

Many sales are lost by getting level locked

Spend too much time with low-level management early in the sales cycle, and you risk becoming level locked. The sooner you call upstairs, the less chance you will have of getting level locked. Without question, the most effective way to avoid getting level locked is to meet with Senior Executives in the first place. An inability to extricate yourself from a level locked situation is a common reason for losing the sale.

No Top Management Calls

To sell successfully, someone representing the selling organization must meet with Senior Executives of the buying organization.

Knowing the language of Senior Executives and how to talk to them is key to winning the business. If you come from a technical background, you might be in your element during technical discussions with low-level management, but this will rarely win you the business. Besides, you're setting yourself up for getting level locked.

> **Know the language of the approver**

If you find yourself avoiding high-level calls, consider studying financial business books, or take a business course to become conversant in the language of the approver. Many sales professionals earn MBAs in their early or mid selling careers or obtain business degrees by correspondence on the Internet or by attending monthly classes while holding down a full-time sales position. Salespeople who have not acquired the ability to communicate effectively with Senior Executives will not win many sales.

Business Issues Not Understood

Your major goal during these sales calls is to discover the corporate pain. You may think you understand the prospects' pain, but it is equally important that the prospect knows you do. To accomplish this, engage in active listening: paraphrasing the problem or situation just described.

No Reference Selling

Orders are sometimes won on the basis of an outstanding reference. Setting up a meeting or telephone call at the right time between the approver and a Senior Executive of one of your customers might be just what is needed to win the sale. A lack of great references can lose the order.

Not Responding to Requests

In today's busy workplace, people don't have time to return phone calls or reply to e-mails. Sales professionals who establish a reputation for responding quickly to requests from prospects will have an edge over those who don't. Try to return phone calls and e-mails to your prospects within twenty-four hours.

Not Demonstrating Your Capabilities

Some products require a demonstration or benchmark to win the sale. Ask yourself the question:

"Have I earned the right to demonstrate my product?"

If the answer is yes, then demo, but do so in the context of addressing the prospect's corporate pain.

Not Involving Your Senior Management

Many sales managers want to discuss your sales strategies with you. The availability of an experienced sales manager to help you brainstorm sales strategies can be very helpful. They may even come up with new ideas to close the order.

When a prospect requests a Senior Executive or manager from your company to assure them that they will be well supported, regard it as a positive, because it affords another opportunity to meet Senior Executives in the buying organization.

A sales professional had been calling for nearly a year on a Southeast Asian airline. The local sales team had done a great job proposing a solution, but there was one last hurdle. They discovered the airline would not issue a purchase order until its chairman received personal assurance from a Senior Executive that all the necessary support would be available. The vice president of sales flew 5,000 miles to have this meeting, which lasted fifteen minutes. Two weeks later, the two firms completed a multi-million dollar sale. It wouldn't have happened without this meeting.

Incorrect Handling of the RFP

Almost always, the RFP requires that all bids be submitted and receipted by the prospect at a specific time. Miss the deadline and your proposal will be rejected. If you have to deliver your proposal on the due date, allow time for traffic congestion.

A salesperson was in the elevator passing the 10th floor when he heard the purchasing department's bell ring on the 12th floor, indicating the bids were closed. His proposal was rejected because it was thirty seconds late.

If you are responding to an RFP, it is prudent to have another person from your company verify that your proposal has addressed all the mandatory requirements.

A principal bidder once lost a five-year purchase agreement with a large multinational company by not addressing a mandatory requirement of the RFP. This resulted in the company missing out on the sale of thousands of personal computers valued at millions of dollars. The sales professional should have had other people from his company vet the proposal to verify that all the mandatory requirements had been addressed. A costly mistake for missing one mandatory requirement!

28. Lost Order Report

Although sales professionals do not like completing administrative reports, a lost order report helps them stay in the top 20% club. Hopefully, you won't have to use such a form very often.

Suppose you have been working for six weeks on a proposal with your technical support team. Your proposal has been submitted, you believe that you are positioned to win the order, and your prospect resides in the last phase of the FUNNEL. Several weeks after submitting the proposal, you are informed that the order was awarded to a competitor. You are devastated. Something went wrong, and you as the account manager must take responsibility and determine why to ensure the mistakes are not repeated. This is why you write a lost order report. The information you need is available from your coaches and those Senior Executives in the prospect's organization with whom you have had a good working relationship.

"Bill, we've had a long and open relationship during the past eight months, and I would appreciate it if you could share with me why we lost your business."

Document the reasons, and share them with your sales team and sales management at a short debriefing meeting. That way everyone will learn from the experience. Be cautious not to blame others for losing the sale, because ultimately, it was your responsibility. "The buck stops here." When you win the order, you get the recognition and the big commission check; when you lose the order, you get to assume the responsibility.

Lost order reports prevent the repetition of mistakes

The lost order report should be no longer than a page, and should describe exactly what went wrong and how it can be avoided. It should be done only for prospects lost near the bottom of the FUNNEL. I know one top sales producer who had to write only five lost order reports in his thirty-year selling career. The good news about conducting this analysis is that it minimizes the chances of making the same mistake twice.

29. Key Points

- Corporate pain is the obstacle a prospect must overcome to solve a corporate problem.

- Successful sales professionals match their solutions to solve the corporate pain.

- Self-interests are requirements that benefit a person's life.

- Successful sales professionals understand the self-interests of each DMP member.

- Face-to-face sales calls build trust.

- Determining corporate pain and self-interest comes from building trust.

- Solution selling is about discovering the corporate pain and self-interests before pitching a solution.

- Successful selling to corporations requires solution selling.

- Senior Executives are usually your best source for discovering corporate pain.

- Watch constantly for introductions to Senior Executives.

- Don't write the proposal until you have verified a budget is in place and know its upper limits.

- The approver is the final authority to purchase your products.

- Be conversant in the language of the approver.

- Make sure you or someone representing your company meets with the approver.

- Your most important task is to persuade the approver to become your advocate.

- Understanding the decision-making process (DMP) is key to winning the sale.

- Develop at least one coach per prospect.

- Know where consultants are playing a role in the DMP, as they can exert a significant influence.

- Have a realistic and specific sales objective for each prospect.

- Cost of ownership analysis is a tool to win the sale without discussing the competition.

- Have one or more specific objectives for each sales call.

- Use a written agenda for each sales call.

- Call reports trigger new ideas. Write a short, concise call report immediately after each sales call.

- Register the "Rules for Asking Questions" into your subconscious.

- Earn the right to submit an unsolicited proposal when appropriate.

- Initiate a joint implementation plan with your prospects near the middle of the sales cycle.

- To avoid getting level locked, call high in the first place.

- No objections = no sale!

- Use the FUNNEL system as your planning tool to join the top 20% club.

Notes

Notes

PART 4:
FUNNEL DESIGN WORKSHOP

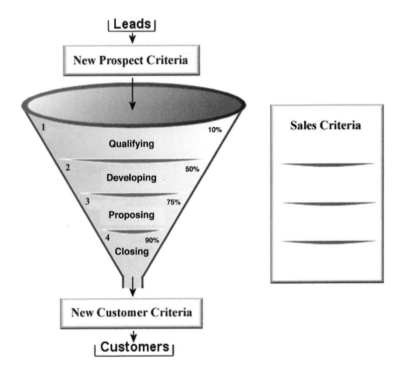

30. Ten-Step FUNNEL Design Workshop

This easy-to-use ten-step FUNNEL Design Workshop provides your company with the tools necessary to customize its FUNNEL system. Four deliverables will emerge from this FUNNEL Design Workshop.

- Customized FUNNEL template

- Ideal sales process

- Balanced FUNNEL

- Customized accurate sales forecast

A sales force will adopt a FUNNEL system and continue to use it, providing the system is on-line and easy to use. This workshop utilizes a four-Phase FUNNEL because it is by far the most common.

STEP 1: Choose FUNNEL Design Team

To select the best design team, include sales management, a number of top sales performers, and a computer specialist with expertise in Web-based products, CRM, or other appropriate software. Small companies might include the entire sales force. Structuring the design team in this way ensures valid sales input into the design. One company's design team consisted of the VP of sales and the seven district sales managers. Several years later, the company is still using the same FUNNEL system successfully.

> Sales management and selected sales professionals must be on the design team

STEP 2: Determine New Prospect Criteria

The purpose of the new prospect criteria is to create a filter that converts leads into new prospects (Figure 20). This filter is located above the FUNNEL, and it establishes your corporate standard for all new prospects entering the top of the FUNNEL.

> The new prospect criteria is the filter used to convert leads into prospects

New Prospect Criteria	Status
Reviewed website/ researched company	X
Credit check confirmed	X
Payment history satisfactory	X
Financially strong (balance sheet)	X
Face-to-face meeting(s)	
NDA signed	X
Sense of urgency	X
Verifies a possible fit	
Technical expertise available	
Local decision making	

Figure 20 Suggested New Prospect Criteria

No prospects should appear in the top of the FUNNEL until the new prospect criteria have been satisfied as shown by a checkmark in the status column. The new prospect criteria consist of up to a dozen criteria and the consensus of the design team in a brainstorming session. Each company should customize its new prospect criteria.

The design team defines the new prospect criteria that best reflect the company's requirements, listed in order of intended execution. By conducting this step rigorously, you ensure a high standard for new prospects entering the FUNNEL.

Figure 21
Four-Phase FUNNEL

> The complexity of the sales process determines the number of Phases needed

STEP 3: Choose Number of Phases

The complexity of the sales process determines the number of Phases required. The largest FUNNEL I've seen had seven, but a three- or four-Phase FUNNEL seems to be the norm. Let's assume you have selected a four-Phase FUNNEL (Figure 21). You'll confirm the validity of this assumption in Step 6. The design team starts by assigning sequential Phase numbers, with Phase 1 located at the top of the FUNNEL. The remaining three Phases are numbered sequentially from top to bottom, Phase 4 becoming the last Phase, located at the bottom of the FUNNEL.

STEP 4: Choose Phase Names

Your design team chooses the Phase names best suited to your company. These names may not necessarily be the examples used below (Figure 22).

Phase #	Three-Phase FUNNEL	Four-Phase FUNNEL	Five-Phase FUNNEL
1	Qualifying	Qualifying	Qualifying
2	Proposing	Developing	Presenting
3	Closing	Proposing	Developing
4		Closing	Proposing
5			Closing

Figure 22 Suggested Phase Names

Phase 1

Most companies name Phase 1 the Qualifying Phase, as it is here that the sales professional identifies the prospect's needs. The Qualifying Phase is located at the top of the FUNNEL.

Phase 2

In four-Phase FUNNELS, Phase 2 is often labeled the Developing Phase because the sales professionals are developing the coaches, determining who is involved in the DMP group, identifying the approver, and conducting presentations and demonstrations.

Phase 3

Many companies call Phase 3 the Proposing Phase because the last criterion in this Phase is usually referred to as "proposal submitted". The proposal is not written until sales criteria found in previous Phases such as "requirements known" and "funding available" are satisfied.

Phase 4

The last Phase is often referred to as the Closing Phase because the last criterion is typically "order received." The Closing Phase is located at the bottom of the FUNNEL.

STEP 5: Determine Sales Criteria

Let's review the roles of two key players in the DMP before determining the sales criteria.

Coaches

Coaches may be located inside or outside the prospect's organization but they must satisfy two criteria:

*   the coach has credibility with the prospect's organization

*   the sales professional has credibility with the coach

It can take a long time to develop a coach. Astute sales professionals are looking for candidates to fulfill this role starting with their first prospecting call. They try not to limit themselves to one coach per prospect, particularly for larger sales. It is the coach who helps sales professionals understand the DMP during the selling process. Your coach may suggest who you should call on next, identify the approver, and alert you to minefields. Rarely does a salesperson close a sale without a coach's help. Outside consultants often make great coaches. During my thirty-year selling career, I have yet to obtain a sale without the assistance of at least one coach.

Approver

The approver is the final approving authority to purchase your products. It may be a person, a committee, or a board, but there is only one final approving authority. Anyone claiming this status but stating that they have to pass the decision upwards is not really the approver.

Sales Criteria

The design team determines what sales criteria are needed during the selling process. The leader solicits from the team the sales criteria previously used to close sales. This is not a traditional brainstorming session, as the team should focus only on sales activities successfully used in the past. Record each sales criteria on flip charts once consensus is reached, allowing adequate discussion time on the validity of each sales criterion. Within two hours, the design team will have listed twenty to fifty validated sales criteria.

Requirements known	Product fit confirmed
Applications defined	Funding available
Buying cycle stage known	Presentation/demo given
Approver identified	Sales objective defined
Other persons to meet identified	Competitors' activities known
Coaches identified	References requested
Buying criteria quantified	Coaches developed
DMP understood	Delivery dates known
Exact budget known	Approver met
Prospect knows its needs understood	Joint implementation plan initiated
Technical requirements satisfied	Benchmark completed satisfactorily
ROI requirements can be satisfied	Objections addressed satisfactorily
Presentation given to approver	Approver on-side
Prospect has contacted references	Head office visited
Proposal submitted	Prospect has contacted references
On short list	Order received
Thank you letter sent to approver	T & C negotiations underway

Figure 23 Four-Phase FUNNEL – Sales Criteria Determination

Let's assume that your design team has created a list of thirty-four sales criteria on the flip charts (Figure 23). The composite sales criteria you develop are unique to your company, but many will be common to other companies. Sales criteria recorded on the flip charts are rarely listed in the order in which they will be executed. Place the flip charts on the wall with masking tape to allow the team to view the sales criteria. After the design team has exhausted its sources of sales criteria, the next step is to fit each sales criterion onto new flip charts representing the four Phases.

STEP 6: Allocate Sales Criteria to Each Phase

> The number of Phases becomes apparent as sales criteria are placed in the Phases

Remember the four-Phase FUNNEL selected in Step 3. Now you are ready to allocate each criterion from Figure 23 into the most appropriate Phase (Figure 24). As you post these sales criteria, it becomes apparent whether the original choice was correct. When the sales process differs from what was originally envisaged, this is the time to increase or reduce the number of Phases. In this example, you are lucky, because all the sales criteria fit nicely into a four-Phase FUNNEL.

Phase 1 - Qualifying	Phase 2 - Developing
1. Application identified	9. Product presentation/demo given
2. Product fit confirmed	10. Buying criteria quantified
3. Buying cycle stage known	11. Competitors' activities known
4. Funding available	12. Approver met
5. Requirements known	13. DMP understood
6. Coaches identified	14. Coaches developed
7. Other persons to meet identified	15. Exact budget known
8. Approver identified	16. References requested
	17. Sales objective defined

Phase 3 - Proposing	Phase 4 - Closing
18. Technical requirements satisfied	30. T & C negotiations underway
19. Delivery dates known	31. On short list
20. Benchmark completed satisfactorily	32. Approver on-side
21. Joint implementation plan initiated	33. Order received
22. Prospect has contacted references	34. Thank you letter sent to approver
23. Prospect knows its needs understood	
24. Head office visited	
25. Reference sites visited	
26. ROI requirements can be satisfied	
27. Presentation given to approver	
28. Proposal submitted	
29. Objections addressed satisfactorily	

Figure 24 Four-Phase FUNNEL – Sales Criteria Allocation

Your design team should use separate flip charts for each Phase so each of the thirty-four sales criteria can be posted onto the appropriate flip chart. There must be consensus on the Phase into which sales criteria must be placed.

STEP 7: Sort Sales Criteria Chronologically

Phase 1 – Qualifying	Planned Date	Actual Date
Requirements known		
Application identified		
Product fit confirmed		
Buying cycle stage known		
Approver identified		
Other persons to meet identified		
Coaches identified		
Funding available		
Phase 2 – Developing		
Buying criteria quantified		
References requested		
Sales objective defined		
Coaches developed		
Approver met		
DMP understood		
Exact budget known		
Product presentation & demo given		
Competitors' activities known		
Phase 3 – Proposing		
Technical requirements satisfied		
Prospect knows its needs understood		
Benchmark completed satisfactorily		
ROI requirements can be satisfied		
Delivery dates known		
Presentation given to approver		
Prospect has contacted references		
Head office visited		
Reference sites visited		
Joint implementation plan initiated		
Objections addressed satisfactorily		
Proposal submitted		
Phase 4 – Closing		
On short list		
Approver on-side		
T&C negotiations underway		
Order received		
Thank you letter sent to approver		

Figure 25 Four-Phase FUNNEL – Sales Criteria

The cumulative sales
criteria approximates the
ideal sales process

The design team's next step is to sort the sales criteria within each Phase logically and in chronological order (Figure 25). This two-stage process of first assigning each sales criterion to a specific Phase (Step 6) and then sorting criteria within each Phase (Step 7) results in a close representation of your company's ideal sales process.

Sorting the sales criteria within each Phase requires more discussion and consensus. For example, the criterion "requirements known" should always precede the criterion "demo given" or "benchmark completed," as it is far better to demonstrate or benchmark in the context of knowing your prospects' requirements.

The criterion "exact budget known" should always precede the criterion "proposal submitted" to avoid wasting time writing proposals when insufficient funds are available. The sales criterion "thank you letter sent to approver" is a thoughtful activity that often gets overlooked by the sales professional in the excitement of obtaining the order. It can be posted as the last sales criterion in the closing phase because it logically follows "order received."

Create two columns beside the sales criteria column, one entitled "planned date" and the other, "actual date" (Figure 25). The "planned date" column assists the sales professional in planning sales strategy and forecasting when the sale will close.

STEP 8: Assign Percentage Probability to Each Phase

Each subsequent Phase
should be assigned a
higher percentage
probability

Assign each subsequent Phase a higher percentage probability for winning the business, because more sales criteria have been satisfied (Figure 26). Percentage probabilities are not derived from a mathematical model, but are based on the number and composition of the sales criteria within a given Phase. What percentage probability should be assigned to each Phase is the next question.

Phase #	Three-Phase FUNNEL	Four-Phase FUNNEL	Five-Phase FUNNEL
1	Qualifying – 10%	Qualifying – 10%	Qualifying – 10%
2	Proposing – 50%	Developing – 50%	Presenting – 40%
3	Closing – 90%	Proposing – 75%	Developing – 50%
4		Closing – 90%	Proposing – 75%
5			Closing – 90%

Figure 26 Suggested Percentage Probabilities

New prospects entering the top of the FUNNEL might satisfy only the new prospect criteria and none of the sales criteria in Phase 1. In this worst case scenario, consider using a percentage probability for Phase 1 as low as 10%. Although some companies still choose up to 25%, your design team should determine what percentage probability is realistic for your company.

By the time your prospect has filtered down to Phase 4, at least twenty-nine of the thirty-four sales criteria have been satisfied (Figure 24). For this reason, the percentage probability for Phase 4 may be as high as 90%.

Now you are ready to choose your percentage probabilities for Phases 2 and 3. Your choice of the percentage probability for these Phases is based on the number and composition of the sales criteria. If a significant number of sales criteria have been placed into either of these two Phases, you might wish to assign a higher percentage probability than that suggested in Figure 26. For example, in Phase 2 you might choose 60% instead of the suggested 50%.

The more thought you give to assigning percentage probabilities, the more accurate the sales forecast.

> The more thought you give to assigning percentage probabilities, the more accurate the sales forecast

STEP 9: Determine New Customer Criteria

Once the sale is closed, there are always a number of important, internal post-sale activities requiring action. Your design team should develop yet another filter, one referred to as the new customer criteria and located below the FUNNEL (Figure 27).

Figure 27 Suggested New Customer Criteria

New Customer Criteria	Status
Review purchase order or agreement	X
Book order	X
Order acknowledged	X
Hand off to technical support team	
Obtain permission for press release	
Schedule project kick-off meeting	

The design team should customize the new customer criteria. As before, denote completion of each sales activity by applying a checkmark to the status column.

STEP 10: Design The Balanced FUNNEL

The Balanced FUNNEL shows the number of prospects required to achieve quota

A balanced FUNNEL is one populated with a sufficient number of prospects in each Phase to allow the sales professional to consistently achieve or exceed quota (Figure 28).

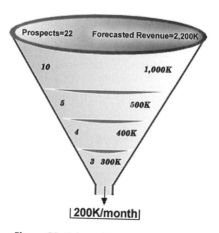

Figure 28 Balanced Four-Phase FUNNEL

Each sales professional will compute how their balanced four-Phase FUNNEL should be populated with prospects to consistently achieve or exceed quota.

An example is shown for Tony Smith, a sales professional, based on his monthly quota of $200K. Historically, the sales cycle is six months. The design team selected the percentage probabilities shown in Figure 29. The parameters used in this calculation are:

Annual quota: $2.4M
Sales cycle: six months
Sales cycle quota: $1.2M
Monthly sales quota: $200K
Average revenue value per prospect: $100K

Phase #	Percentage Probability (%)	Calculated Revenue ($K) Monthly Sales Quota/PP	Revenue Forecast Needed($K)	# of Prospects Needed
1	20	200/.2 = 1,000	1,000	10
2	40	200/.4 = 500	500	5
3	60	200/.6 = 333	400	4
4	90	200/.9 = 222	300	3
			Total: 2,200	Total: 22

Figure 29 Balanced Four-Phase FUNNEL – Calculated Revenue Forecast Needed

The revenue forecast needed in each Phase to achieve monthly revenues of $200K encompasses two steps. The first step involves computing the calculated revenue by dividing the monthly sales quota by the percentage probability of that Phase. The second step requires rounding up each calculated revenue to the nearest higher integer of $100K, as the latter figure represents the nominated average revenue value per prospect. The calculated revenue in Phase 4 is $222K. This is rounded up to $300K to reflect the addition of one more average sale. The $300K represents the revenue forecast needed in Phase 4. We then compute the number of prospects needed in each

The revenue forecast needed reflects the weighted effect of the percentage probabilities

Phase by dividing the revenue forecast needed by the average revenue value per prospect. In this example, the number of prospects needed in Phase 4 is three, obtained by dividing $300K by $100K.

In order to generate consistent monthly revenue of $200K, Tony's balanced four-Phase FUNNEL would require twenty-two prospects with an average value of $100K and a total revenue forecast needed of $2,200K (Figure 29).

One limitation with this model is that the revenue forecast needed is seldom known for all the prospects in Phase 1. The only objective the sales professional can realistically achieve is to ensure there are the required number of prospects needed in Phase 1. In Tony's example, ten prospects should be residing in Phase 1.

Tony's actual forecast from the prospects in Phases 2, 3, and 4 must equal or exceed the revenue forecast needed for each of those Phases.

Now that the four-Phase FUNNEL has been designed, Tony can load his prospects into the accurate sales forecast (Figure 30) using the FUNNEL template (Figure 31) as the instrument.

31. Creating an Accurate Sales Forecast

Tony's accurate sales forecast template has been formatted to reflect his actual FUNNEL status, and also displays the parameters of his balanced four-Phase FUNNEL (Figure 30). Tony must confirm the sales forecast and the forecast date for each of his prospects.

Sales forecast in Phases 2, 3 and 4 must equal revenue forecast needed

Remember Tony's monthly sales quota was $200K. He can achieve or exceed this as long as the sales forecast for Phases 2, 3, and 4 equals or exceeds the $1,200K revenue forecast needed, and there are at least twenty-two prospects in the four Phases (Figure 30). The current status of Tony's

Sales Professional: Tony Smith			Forecast Date: April 30, 200X		
Balanced Forecast	Actual # of Prospects	Code	Prospect Name	Sales Forecast($K)	Forecast Date
Phase 1	1	CAN	The ARC Group		
	2	EMC	Electro-Meters Company		
	3	MTC	Micro-Tech Computers		Nov.
	4	AC	Artemis PR & Design		August
	5	REL	Reliable Controls ™		August
	6	WCT	WCG International		August
	7	ABC 2	ABC Company #2	110	July
	8				
	9				
10 prospects	10				
$1,000K	Total=7			Total=110	
Phase 2	11	KCS	Kinetic Computer Solutions	125	July
	12	ABC 1	ABC Company #1	95	July
	13	OSI 2	Open Solutions Inc. #2	75	July
	14	PBS	Peak Business Systems	110	July
	15	BDI	Brookdale International	600	June
5 prospects	16	MM2	Mardon Marketing #2	100	June
$500K	Total=6			Total=1,105	
Phase 3	17	ISSC	Infinte Source Systems Corp.	105	June
	18	XYZ 2	XYZ Company #2	84	June
	19	OSI 1	Open Solutions Inc. #1	102	June
4 prospects	20	ADT	Addonics Technologies	105	May
$400K	Total=4			Total=396	
Phase 4	21	EEE	Triple E Training Inc.	113	May
	22	MM 1	Mardon Marketing #1	106	May
3 prospects	23	XYZ 1	XYZ Company #1	99	May
$300K	Total=3			Total=318	
Number of prospects=20				Total Actual Forecast=1,929	
Needed prospects=22			Revenue Forecast Needed=1,200 (Phases 2, 3, and 4)		

Figure 30 Four-Phase FUNNEL – Accurate Sales Forecast Template

FUNNEL shows that he has seven prospects in Phase 1, but he requires ten. You can expect Tony to intensify his prospecting program to add three additional prospects in the next several weeks. He has ensured he can still achieve his quota in the month that Brookdale International ($600K) may exit the FUNNEL sideways. This is why he has six prospects in Phase 2 even though his balanced FUNNEL requires only five prospects.

Applying percentage probability as presented in this FUNNEL Design Workshop always results in a more accurate sales forecast than one that applies the same or no weight to every prospect.

32. Introducing the FUNNEL to the Sales Force

This FUNNEL template illustrates where prospect ABC 1 is in the sales process (Figure 31). Once the design team has customized the FUNNEL system, it should be formally launched to the sales force in a way similar to how product training is introduced.

If the template is generated from the accurate sales forecast (Figure 30), the software should insert the code used for the prospect's name inside the small FUNNEL diagram shown in Figure 31. The software should also insert the "date" of the FUNNEL template and the "name" of the sales professional as shown at the top of the template.

The prospect ABC 1 will advance to Phase 3 as soon as "exact budget known" and "presentation/demo given" in Phase 2 are satisfied.

The sales professional should complete a new FUNNEL template whenever they activate a new lead. Each new FUNNEL template will portray the status of the new prospect criteria, sales criteria and the new customer criteria. The FUNNEL template allows the sales professional to review

Hyperlink the accurate sales forecast with each FUNNEL template

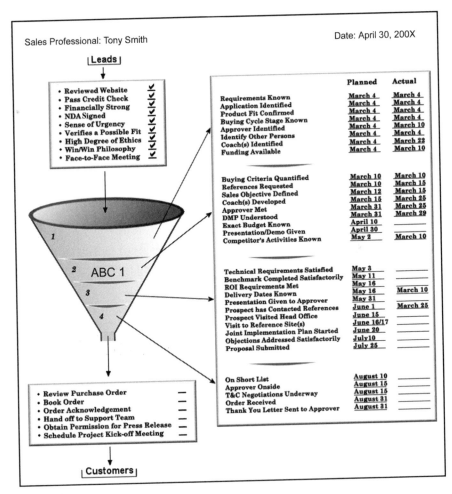

Figure 31 Four-Phase FUNNEL Template

The design team has now created the FUNNEL template (Figure 31) built from the following:

- Suggested New Prospect Criteria (Figure 20)
- Four-Phase FUNNEL (Figure 21)
- Four-Phase FUNNEL – Sales Criteria (Figure 25)
- Suggested New Customer Criteria (Figure 27)

where each prospect is in the sales cycle and determine the next sales criteria requiring action. A hyperlink in both directions should link each prospect listed in the accurate sales forecast and its corresponding FUNNEL template. Have your accurate sales forecast and FUNNEL templates for all your prospects with you all the time.

Computing Your Balanced FUNNEL

Sales professionals must compute their own balanced FUNNELS, substituting their parameters in the straightforward process described in Step 10.

On-line FUNNEL System

> A successful FUNNEL system must be on-line and easy to use

The FUNNEL system will be used only if it is on-line and easy to use. Using software products such as CRM, your FUNNEL system can be up and running quickly. It is very important to design your FUNNEL template before implementing the on-line version.

Managing Your FUNNEL System

The accurate sales forecast template (Figure 30) contains the parameters of the balanced FUNNEL as well as the actual status of each prospect in the FUNNEL. Now is the time for Tony to manage his FUNNEL system. He should begin by balancing his FUNNEL because it is short by three Phase 1 prospects. He should quickly add three more prospects to satisfy Phase 1 requirements.

Sales professionals need to achieve balanced FUNNELS within a realistic time frame. Reaching this steady-state condition in a new sales territory can take six months to a year. This time frame depends largely on the complexity of the selling process. Once you've completed three or four monthly FUNNELS, you can often forecast when your FUNNEL will be balanced.

The sales professional must ensure that the actual revenue forecast of all prospects within each Phase, except for Phase 1, equals or exceeds the revenue forecast needed. It is not uncommon to have one prospect whose targeted revenue exceeds the revenue forecast needed for an entire Phase. In this situation, the sales professional must ensure there are sufficient prospects in that Phase to achieve quota should this large prospect be lost. If it remains in his FUNNEL, Tony has the opportunity to significantly exceed his quota in June. Astute sales professionals will replenish their FUNNELS with three or four new prospects in the weeks following a sale.

Now that the design team has created the FUNNEL in the form of the accurate sales forecast (Figure 30) and the FUNNEL template (Figure 31), Tony can verify that his existing prospects still qualify by passing them through the new prospect criteria. Previously perceived prospects must satisfy the new prospect criteria to remain a prospect; otherwise, they revert to being leads or are abandoned. Similarly, as each new lead passes the new prospect criteria, it too becomes a new prospect.

Next, measure the reclassified prospects and all new prospects against the sales criteria in order to assign them to the appropriate Phase. Occasionally, sales professionals can satisfy the new prospect criteria and Phase 1 sales criteria on the first prospecting call, thus converting the lead directly into a Phase 2 prospect.

Your last task is to move the prospects through the FUNNEL until they exit the bottom and become customers. As you evolve your sales strategy for each prospect, you will identify dates by which you can reasonably expect to satisfy each sales criterion. Place these dates beside their respective sales criterion under the "planned" column, and as each sales criterion is satisfied, place the date beside the respective sales criterion under the "actual" column. You are now ready to determine into which Phase each prospect should be placed. To move each prospect into the next Phase, all sales criteria in the preceding Phases must have been satisfied. The advantage of this approach is that it highlights which sales criteria remain outstanding. The second last sales criterion in the final Phase is "order received". On the date the order is received, the prospect moves out the bottom of the FUNNEL and becomes a customer.

Mail thank you letter within a day of obtaining the order

The thank you letter is not really a sales criterion, but placing it last reminds you to take this act of courtesy as soon as you obtain the order. Avoid sending e-mail, as a paper thank you letter has far more impact and tends to be shown to others in the customer's organization. It should be on your letterhead and signed by a Senior Executive or your president. Some companies place these letters on file. You never know who might read it at a later date.

33. The Two Indispensable Sales Tools

The accurate sales forecast and FUNNEL templates are your two indispensable sales tools

By now you know the two indispensable sales tools of the sales professional.

The Accurate Sales Forecast (Figure 30)

The accurate sales forecast is indispensable because it represents the sales professional's entire sales program. It tells you which prospects need your attention next. Make your updated accurate sales forecast readily available on your computer, laptop, or tablet, and insert a hard copy on the inside front cover of your notebook. Before you know it you will have your entire sales program memorized.

Place each prospect in the appropriate Phase of your FUNNEL. Ensure that the forecast in each Phase equals or exceeds the actual revenue needed and you are well positioned to achieve quota.

A start-up company attempting to obtain a second round of financing will have a major problem if first-year sales are nowhere near target. If the first-year plan is to close $2 million in sales, and the company closes only $500,000, a second round of financing will be difficult to obtain. The investment community won't have confidence in the company achieving future sales projections. This could result in your company going bankrupt or in replacing all or part of the sales force. This is a good reason to use a weighted accurate sales forecast.

The FUNNEL Template (Figure 31)

The FUNNEL template is the other indispensable sales tool. Every time sales professionals activate a new lead, they need to create a new FUNNEL template, which they activate just before the first prospecting call, as it vividly reminds them of the new prospect criteria. It is easy to update the FUNNEL template the same time they complete the call report.

Taken together, the accurate sales forecast and FUNNEL templates go a long way to assisting sales professionals in deciding at a glance which prospects require attention (accurate sales forecast) and which sales activities require action (FUNNEL template).

It can't get any simpler than this.

34. Key Points

- This ten-step FUNNEL Design Workshop is easily implemented and delivers:
  - A customized FUNNEL template
  - Balanced FUNNELS
  - An optimized sales process
  - An accurate sales forecast

- The balanced FUNNEL depicts the number of prospects needed in each Phase to achieve quota.

- Include sales management and selected sales professionals on the design team.

- To design your FUNNEL system, conduct a one-day workshop.

- Sales planning systems must be easy to use and on-line.

- The cumulative sales criteria of all Phases closely approximates your ideal sales process.

- Automate your FUNNEL system with software after you have developed the system.

- The new prospect criteria establishes your corporate standard for all new prospects entering the top of the FUNNEL.

- The number of Phases needed is a function of the complexity of your sales process.

- A three- or four-Phase FUNNEL meets the needs of most small to mid-sized companies.

- Applying percentage probability always results in a more accurate sales forecast than applying the same weight to every prospect.

- Derive your company's sales criteria from those used to close previous sales.

- Assign a low percentage probability to prospects residing in Phase 1.

- Because more sales criteria have been satisfied as the prospect moves down the FUNNEL, each subsequent Phase is assigned a higher percentage probability.

- Compute revenue forecast needed for each Phase using percentage probabilities.

- The sales forecast for the Phases must equal or exceed the revenue forecast needed with the exception of Phase 1.

- Because budgets are unknown for many Phase 1 prospects, it is more realistic to set the number of prospects needed as the Phase 1 target.

- The accurate sales forecast and the FUNNEL templates are the sales professionals' two indispensable sales tools.

Notes

Notes

EPILOGUE

Don, a sales professional with Hewlett Packard in the 1970s, had been calling on a university on the east coast for six months, and had a prospect valued at $350,000 near the bottom of his FUNNEL. About this time, Dr. Ron MacKinnon, the chairman of the selection committee, informed him that although they had been considering the HP solution, the competitor had recently made two significant announcements.

- Their newly announced computer system was superior to the Hewlett Packard product.
- They had heard from reliable sources that HP was not staying in the computer business.

The chairman went on to state that the competitor had invited them to visit its factory in Detroit and its software development center in Santa Barbara.

The following week, Don was visiting the HP factory when he spotted HP President Bill Hewlett. He introduced himself and said, "Bill, I had expected to book a large order from an east coast university this quarter, but they have been told recently by the competitor that HP is not staying in the computer business. If I can arrange for their chairman to meet with you, would you be willing to tell him that you are committed to HP staying in the computer business?"

Bill replied, "Absolutely, Don."

Don then phoned the chairman and asked him if he would like to meet Bill Hewlett while in California visiting the competition. Don stated that Bill would confirm that HP was committed to staying in the computer business. The chairman said he would very much like to have this meeting.

Don's sales management was delighted that he had set up this very important Friday morning meeting with Bill Hewlett, and insisted that he stay in the Bay area for the weekend to host the chairman. His sales manager's last words were to make certain the chairman got on the plane Monday morning, so he wouldn't be returning to Santa Barbara for another meeting.

What was to be a meeting with Bill Hewlett, the chairman, and Don quickly expanded when three middle-level HP factory managers somehow managed to include themselves. After Don made the introductions, Bill immediately said to the chairman, "Ron, I understand that you come from a beautiful part of the country. In fact, I have a friend who worked with me on radar research during the war now living there. He has been trying to get me to visit him for some time now. The chairman replied, "Perhaps you could time this visit with the commissioning of our new HP system."

This was a great way to start, as up to that point, there had been no signals that HP might win this business. After a lengthy pause, Bill turned to the HP middle-level managers and asked, "How in the world are we going to support this installation in the Northeast when our nearest support facility is 1,000 miles away?" One of the managers replied, "Well, Bill, we've just designed a remote diagnostic capability that includes hardware and software pop-up panels permitting our systems engineers to run remote diagnostics."

Bill replied, "I understand that this capability has been delayed for nearly a year." His words punctured the euphoria, but by the end of the meeting, Bill did state that he was personally committed to HP staying in the computer business.

During the weekend, Don and the chairman visited many Bay area tourism sites. Late Sunday afternoon, as they were leaving a winery in Napa Valley, the chairman said,

"Don, you don't even know why I am going to order from HP, do you?"

"No, I don't Ron."

"Don, any company that has a president like yours, who is more interested in ensuring HP customers are properly supported than in just obtaining the sale is the only kind of company with which I want to do business."

The following month, the university booked an order for a $350,000 system, and a few years later they ordered a second system for $400,000. Shortly after receiving the first order, Don wrote Bill a thank you letter telling him they had won the order. About a month later, Don received a congratulatory letter from Bill Hewlett saying to feel free to approach him directly any time he needed help.

Despite all the tips and guidelines presented in KEEPING THE FUNNEL FULL, nothing is more important than your prospects and customers knowing you care about them and will do everything in your power to help them achieve success.

AUTHOR'S SUGGESTION

Congratulations! You now have a wonderful set of sales tools to keep you in the top 20% club. May I suggest that you keep this book near your workstation as your indispensable sales tool? For long business trips, why not carry it in your briefcase? I'd enjoy receiving your feedback anytime on how you have benefited from your new sales tool.

Don Thomson

don@keepingthefunnelfull.com

Notes

Notes

GLOSSARY

Approver: A person, committee, or board in the prospect's organization who gives final approval to purchase products.

Accurate sales forecast: A sales forecast using percentage probabilities to determine the revenue forecast needed to achieve or exceed quota.

Balanced FUNNEL: A FUNNEL populated with a sufficient number of prospects in each Phase to consistently achieve or exceed quota.

Coach: A person with whom you have credibility and who has credibility with the buying organization.

Complex sale: A selling situation where more than one person is involved in the decision-making process.

Corporate pain: Refers to obstacles a company must overcome to solve a corporate problem.

Cover off: Having someone representing your company make a face-to-face call on a DMP member.

Customer: An organization that has contracted to purchase your products. Customers reside below the FUNNEL.

Decision-making process (DMP): The process used by corporations to select vendors.

DMP group: The group of persons who play a role in the DMP.

FUNNEL: A FUNNEL shape representing the status of each prospect in the sales cycle.

FUNNEL template: A template integrating the new prospect criteria, sales criteria, and the new customer criteria.

Influencer: A person who influences other members of the DMP group.

Lead: An organization with the potential to become a customer. Leads reside above the FUNNEL.

Level locked: A situation where a low-level manager prevents the sales professional from having access to a high-level manager.

Lost or abandoned order: A prospect exiting the FUNNEL sideways as a result of being lost to the competition or intentionally abandoned.

New customer criteria: Internal activities that require action after an order is received.

New prospect criteria: Activities that convert leads into prospects.

Percentage probability: An index to improve the accuracy of the sales forecast by weighting each Phase by a percentage.

Phase: A logical grouping of sales criteria appearing in chronological order in the FUNNEL.

Products: Goods and services offered for sale or lease.

Prospect: A sales opportunity that satisfies the new prospect criteria. Prospects reside inside the FUNNEL.

Prospect's needs: Comprised of the corporate pain and self-interests of each DMP member.

Prospecting calls: Face-to-face calls needed to convert leads into prospects.

Prospecting process: The process that converts leads into prospects.

Revenue forecast needed: The revenue needed in each Phase to achieve quota.

Selling process: The process that converts prospects into customers.

Sales calls: Face-to-face calls needed to convert a prospect into a customer.

Sales criteria: Activities that allow a prospect to move down to the next Phase.

Sales cycle: The sales process expressed as a function of time.

Screening source: A person who can prevent a meeting with a DMP member.

Self-interest: Those objective and subjective requirements that benefit a person's life.

Solution selling: The level of selling where sales professionals determine the prospect's needs before pitching their products.

Senior Executive: A member of the prospect's executive management team. Successful sales professionals focus on Senior Executives.

Stuck order: A prospect residing near the middle of the FUNNEL for a period of time longer than its normal sales cycle.

INDEX